CHINESE IMAGES OF
THE UNITED STATES

Significant Issues Series
Timely books presenting current CSIS research and analysis of interest to the academic,
business, government, and policy communities.
Managing Editor: Roberta L. Howard

The Center for Strategic and International Studies (CSIS) is a nonprofit, bipartisan
public policy organization established in 1962 to provide strategic insights and practical
policy solutions to decisionmakers concerned with global security. Over the years, it has
grown to be one of the largest organizations of its kind, with a staff of some 200
employees, including more than 120 analysts working to address the changing dynamics
of international security across the globe.

CSIS is organized around three broad program areas, which together enable it to
offer truly integrated insights and solutions to the challenges of global security. First,
CSIS addresses the new drivers of global security, with programs on the international
financial and economic system, foreign assistance, energy security, technology,
biotechnology, demographic change, the HIV/AIDS pandemic, and governance.
Second, CSIS also possesses one of America's most comprehensive programs on U.S.
and international security, proposing reforms to U.S. defense organization, policy, force
structure, and its industrial and technology base and offering solutions to the challenges
of proliferation, transnational terrorism, homeland security, and post-conflict
reconstruction. Third, CSIS is the only institution of its kind with resident experts on all
the world's major populated geographic regions.

CSIS was founded four decades ago by David M. Abshire and Admiral Arleigh Burke.
Former U.S. senator Sam Nunn became chairman of the CSIS Board of Trustees in 1999,
and since April 2000, John J. Hamre has led CSIS as president and chief executive officer.

Headquartered in downtown Washington, D.C., CSIS is a private, tax-exempt,
501(c) 3 institution.

The CSIS Press
Center for Strategic and International Studies
1800 K Street, N.W., Washington, D.C. 20006
Tel: (202) 887-0200 Fax: (202) 775-3199
E-mail: books@csis.org   Web: www.csis.org

CHINESE IMAGES OF THE UNITED STATES

EDITED BY CAROLA McGIFFERT

FOREWORD BY JOHN J. HAMRE

THE CSIS PRESS

**Center for Strategic
and International Studies**

Washington, D.C.

Significant Issues Series, Volume 27, Number 3
© 2005 by Center for Strategic and International Studies
Washington, D.C. 20006
All rights reserved
Printed on recycled paper in the United States of America
Cover design by Robert L. Wiser, Silver Spring, Md.
Cover photograph: Chinese Communist leader Deng Xiaoping wearing
          cowboy hat. © Bettmann/Corbis.

09 08 07 06 05   5 4 3 2 1

ISSN 0736-7136
ISBN 0-89206-465-X

Library of Congress Cataloging-in-Publication Data

Chinese images of the United States / edited by Carola McGiffert ; foreword by
John J. Hamre.
      p. cm. — (Significant issues series ; v. 27, no. 3)
   Includes bibliographical references and index.
   ISBN 0-89206-465-X (pb : alk. paper)
 1. United States—Relations—China. 2. China—Relations—United States. 3. United
States—Foreign public opinion—Chinese. 4. United States—Foreign relations—20th
century. I. McGiffert, Carola. II. Title. III. Series.
   E183.8.C5C5385 2005
   973—dc22
                          2005008394

CONTENTS

FOREWORD

AMERICAN PERCEPTIONS OF CHINA'S RISE

John J. Hamre

BASED ON THE RHETORIC during the 2000 presidential campaign in the United States, many experts predicted that U.S.-China relations were headed for rocky times. Candidate George W. Bush criticized China for its lack of religious freedom, its human rights practices, and its growing military power, and he accused the Clinton administration of engaging in a "strategic partnership" with China that undermined U.S. interests. China, in Bush's view, was not a partner, but a competitor, one that needed to be watched carefully and even contained. This view was supported by Bush's top advisers, many of whom were later appointed to senior positions in his administration.

Yet just three and a half years later, U.S.-China relations were described by Secretary of State Colin Powell as "the best they have been since President Richard Nixon first visited Beijing more than 30 years ago."[1] This represents the growing recognition throughout U.S. society that, while our disagreements with China may be profound, our common interests are equally profound—and growing.

This back and forth in U.S. China policy, both within the Bush administration and over the past 55 years, reflects a larger ambiguity that the American people feel toward China. For Americans, China is full of contradictions. While China has clearly transformed itself since the days of the Cultural Revolution, images of Tiananmen still linger in the American memory. Today, the Chinese people are freer than they ever have been—to live, work, and travel where they want, to dress and act as they please, and, increasingly, to say what they think. Yet, at the same time, China remains a one-party state where corruption remains an enormous challenge and crackdowns on freedom of speech are not uncommon. Hundreds of millions of Chinese have been lifted out of poverty over the past few decades, China's economy is booming, and many are getting rich; yet the poor are getting poorer and there is no safety net underneath them. China is arguably playing an increasingly constructive role in international affairs, yet it continues to strengthen its military capabilities and, in particular, threaten the use of military force against Taiwan.

In short, China's rise, both economic and military, underscores the conflicting feelings that Americans have toward China. The American people are both impressed and unnerved by China's decisive emergence as a major player on the world stage.

Among the policy elite, a few different American perspectives on China can be generalized. First is the view of China as a growing military threat. From this perspective, China is rapidly building up its military, focusing on acquiring high technology and on making its forces more mobile and more nimble. Some Americans believe that China's military modernization is targeted against the United States and that the United States should therefore prepare for an eventual, and possibly inevitable, war with China, most likely over Taiwan. Those who adhere to this line of thought argue that developing a ballistic missile defense capability is critical to containing and defending against China.

A second group of Americans sees China as a rising economic threat. The U.S. economy continues to lose manufacturing jobs to China, and service jobs are increasingly being outsourced to China (and elsewhere) as well. This group focuses on issues like China's currency, which it argues is undervalued and is therefore keeping costs artificially low, its trade barriers and lack of enforcement of World Trade Organization obligations, and its low labor standards.

A strong majority of Americans, however, holds more positive views of China. These Americans see China's rise as a positive development, and encourage China to take a greater leadership role on economic and security issues in the region and globally. They appreciate the benefits of the Chinese market for the U.S. economy and seek to encourage political reform in China over the long term through engagement. They applaud China's cooperation in the war on terrorism. Yet, at the same time, they are deeply concerned about the significant challenges that China faces domestically, from unemployment and a growing regional income gap, to an aging population and HIV/AIDs, to environmental degradation and a lack of an effective social safety net. These Americans who have, on balance, a positive view of China can be divided into two general groups: those who focus on the weighty challenges that China must confront and those who focus on the tremendous success China has achieved to date.

As the shift in policy toward China during the Bush administration suggests, the dominant American view of China is a cautiously positive one. In this view, China is seen as a nation that has, throughout history, risen to meet its challenges. Its leaders are pragmatic and are genuine in their efforts to build a prosperous country that takes care of all its citizens. The Chinese people are entrepreneurial, resilient, and capable of achieving remarkable success even under difficult circumstances.

For its part, the Chinese leadership is pursuing its policies not only pragmatically, but strategically as well, and, as a result, China has burst onto the international stage in a major way. The rest of the world, including the United States, will have to determine how to deal with China's rise, and how our actions and policies toward China can encourage China along a peaceful path or, alternatively, could push China in a more difficult and confrontational direction.

In contrast with China's strategic outlook, the United States has unfortunately taken a very ideological stance on a range of global issues in recent years. For some U.S. policymakers, a more positive image of China is simply designed to win the support of China for U.S. initiatives, like the war on terrorism. This tactical approach to China is not sustainable, however, and the United States must begin to think more strategically about its relationship with a strong—and "risen"—China over the long term. If we do not do so, problems between China and the United States are all but certain to recur, and this time we will be confronting a much stronger China. However, if we can recover a sense of strategic direction and adopt a more pragmatic approach in dealing with China, U.S.-China relations hold great promise.

Note

1. Colin L. Powell, "A Strategy of Partnerships," *Foreign Affairs,* January/February 2004.

PREFACE

Carola McGiffert

WHEN THE *Empress of China* arrived in Canton (today's Guangzhou) in August 1784, Americans officially joined the ranks of the "foreign devils" that China allowed onto its shores. Like the Europeans before them, American traders were kept at arm's length, restricted to special market-places, and not allowed to travel freely around the country. American resources were welcome in China, but American culture was not. Americans accepted the Chinese attitude. "China is the first for greatness, richness, and grandeur of any country ever known," wrote one pioneering sea captain.[1]

EARLY U.S.-CHINA CONTACTS

The early history of U.S. traders and, later, missionaries in China has shaped Chinese images of the United States ever since. Compared with the British, Americans made a favorable first impression. The Chinese perceived American traders as relatively honorable, they saw American missionaries offer social as well as religious services, and the United States—so recently a colony itself—did not appear to have hegemonic aims. As contact between the two nations grew, China began to praise the U.S. political system and the ideals of U.S. leaders such as George Washington. For a short time, in the early 1800s, U.S.-China relations were conducted on largely positive and equal terms. As Hu Guocheng notes in chapter one of this volume, "bilateral nongovernmental trade and people-to-people exchange flourished on the basis of mutual economic benefit and political equality."

Beginning a few decades into the nineteenth century, however, the United States began acting more like a traditional opportunistic power, and Chinese opinions of their American friends soured. During the next century, Washington compelled Beijing to sign unequal treaties such as the Wangxia Treaty (1844), through which U.S.-China relations were officially established. These agreements not only secured greater U.S. access to Chinese land, resources, and goods without giving back much in return, but they also, in the Chinese view, undermined Chinese sovereignty. During the Sino-British Opium War (1839–1842), the United States was seen as following in Britain's footsteps, and concerns grew that the United States, like its European counterparts, did in fact have colonial ambitions. Discrimination against and exploitation of Chinese people in the United States, codified in the Chinese Exclusion Act (1882), also made news in China. As a result, distrust became a dominant sentiment in the bilateral relationship.

Thus, beginning in the mid-nineteenth century, the pendulum of Chinese images of the United States swung from respect to hostility. These sharply contrasting sentiments have been a common thread in U.S-.China relations since the *Empress* sailed into port more than 200 years ago. This collection of essays explores how Chinese perceptions of America and Americans have evolved over the course of modern history, and how those perceptions have influenced U.S.-China relations.

RECENT U.S.-CHINA CONTACTS

Echoes of early positive sentiments between the two countries can be heard today. Although real challenges exist in today's bilateral relationship, there remains a great deal of mutual respect between the two nations. Americans may denounce the Chinese political system, but they marvel at China's ancient culture, its entrepreneurial spirit, and its rapid economic modernization. Chinese people may abhor U.S. foreign policy, but they admire the U.S. political ideals, educational system, and economic prosperity. On a personal level, Chinese and American people respect each other.

Yet the distrust that first developed in the mid-nineteenth century and continued throughout China's "century of shame"—the perceived humiliation the nation experienced at the hands of foreigners beginning during the Opium War and extending until Mao's Communists "stood up" in 1949—also remains a fixture in U.S.-China relations. For example, the U.S. bombing of the Chinese embassy in Belgrade in 1999 was immediately assumed in China to have been deliberate, and no amount of reassurance by the U.S. government that it was a terrible mistake could convince the Chinese people otherwise.

U.S. support for Taiwan, in particular, is widely seen as evidence of hegemonic U.S. policy. Almost to a person, Chinese believe that Taiwan is part of China and that the United States is illegitimately interfering in an internal affair by engaging Taiwan politically (if technically unofficially) as well as selling arms. These actions, in the Chinese mind, undermine Chinese sovereignty and represent a U.S. effort to destabilize China or contain its rise. Taiwan remains a deeply emotional issue for most Chinese, and it continues to be an important lens through which China looks at the United States. As long as Taiwan's political status remains unresolved and as long as the United States tries to maintain an ambiguous status quo, Taiwan will continue to negatively color Chinese images of the United States.

Contradiction.   One of the consistent themes in U.S.-China relations, therefore, is contradiction. The so-called love-hate component of the bilateral relationship has become almost a cliché, but it nonetheless holds true. Opposing yin-yang forces are present in Chinese views of the United States, both yesterday and today, and, as noted by Wang Jisi in chapter two, contradictory images "coexist in the Chinese heart."

This dichotomy can be traced through modern history. In the early twentieth century, Sun Yat-sen, who had spent significant time with U.S. political leaders, presented a positive image of the United States to the Chinese people, one that was soon undermined by the terms of the 1919 Paris peace conference. During World War II, the United States gained Chinese appreciation for its victory against the Japanese, but this positive feeling quickly eroded because of the U.S. policy of anticommunism, which led to U.S. involvement in the wars in Korea and

Vietnam. Rapprochement between China and the United States in the 1970s inspired a Chinese view of America as a land of economic opportunity, a view soon to be overshadowed by a resentment of perceived American cultural and political arrogance after the U.S.-led reaction to the 1989 Tiananmen crackdown.

An excellent survey, conducted by the Institute of American Studies at the Chinese Academy of Social Sciences and discussed in chapter six by Zhao Mei, clearly demonstrates that Chinese people continue to have conflicting images of the United States today. Almost 70 percent of those surveyed responded that they have "mixed views" of the United States; they cited positive views of the high U.S. standard of living and domestic policy and negative views of what was termed hegemonism in international affairs and an imprudent China policy. Many Chinese people sympathized with the United States after the September 11, 2001, attacks while others celebrated the attacks as just punishment for U.S. global aggressiveness and unilateralism. In chapter nine, Cheng Shengluo describes the responses of some Chinese students to the 9/11 attacks; many were "excited," "delighted," and "happy" that the United States had been taken down a notch, and they noted their "admiration" for the "hero" who orchestrated the attacks. While many of these students later expressed regret for their initial reaction, their comments nonetheless reflect a deep resentment of the United States.

Chinese vie to send their children to U.S. universities, and they embrace U.S. popular culture (movies, music, and sports), yet they simultaneously condemn U.S. cultural dominance. Chinese admire U.S. values, yet they resent having those values imposed on them and, according to Lu Jiande in chapter five, view the United States as betraying its "spirit of freedom" and "squandering its political capital." Chinese citizens praise the U.S. legal system but accuse the United States of applying international law in an arbitrary fashion, according to Li Xiaoping in chapter seven. This seesaw of emotions has long been a defining characteristic of the Sino-U.S. relationship.

Differentiation. Another consistent theme in Chinese images of the United States is the differentiation between, on one hand, the American people and their political and economic systems and, on the other hand, the U.S. government. Chinese people typically like American people and admire U.S. democratic institutions and ideals, but they dislike U.S. government policies. In the late eighteenth and early nineteenth centuries, American missionaries were perceived as good-hearted people who sought to help Chinese people; in contrast, the U.S. government was coldhearted and sought to exploit Chinese land and riches. Today, Americans are seen as open-minded and generous, while the U.S. government is perceived as conducting its policies on purely self-interested terms. The U.S.-led war in Iraq is a recent example of U.S. unilateralist policy that has been widely condemned in China.

Self-image. A third theme in Chinese images of the United States is the role of China's self-image. When China feels weak or attacked or when Chinese pride is undermined, China seeks to shift blame elsewhere. This is human nature, of course, and not unique to China. What may be unique to China, however, is a dual superiority-inferiority complex born of centuries of cultural and technological predominance, followed by a steep fall into isolation, followed by political colonization and economic backwardness. In recent decades, China has clearly emerged from that backwardness, but it retains deep scars from its century and a half of subordination and relative obscurity. It seeks to regain its central place in the world order and resents any country that appears to be standing in its way. The Mandarin word for China is *zhongguo*—Middle Kingdom—and that is where China has historically and psychologically placed itself: in the center. The Chinese psyche, shaped by a historical combination of self-aggrandizement and self-pity, in turn shapes China's view of the world and, in particular, the United States.

Ideology also has played a role in shaping Chinese images of the United States, particularly during the twentieth century, although to a decreasing degree with the passage of time. During the Cold War, ideology—buttressed by a tightly controlled propaganda machine—was perhaps the most important determinant of Chinese images of the United States. The United States was a friend of the Kuomintang and a foe of communists worldwide, and its involvement in the Korean and Vietnam wars provided Chinese leaders with ample evidence of U.S.

hegemonic aims. Since the end of the Cold War, communist ideology has become less important, of course, but nonetheless remains a useful tool on occasion.

The ideology of the past 25 years has been less about communism itself than about the legitimacy of the Chinese Communist Party, and the party leadership is not beyond demonizing the United States to rally support among the Chinese people. For example, the Chinese government reportedly did not publicize U.S. apologies after the 1999 embassy bombing and even encouraged students and others to go to the U.S. embassy in Beijing to engage in what devolved into a violent protest. It was politically convenient at that time to promote a negative image of the United States to the Chinese people. After the April 2001 near collision of a Chinese F-7 fighter jet and a U.S. reconnaissance plane, the Chinese government won domestic praise for its perceived tough stance on when to release the U.S. plane and its crew.

CHINESE IMAGES OF THE UNITED STATES

This book builds on a previous CSIS volume, *China in the American Political Imagination* (2003), which offered a collection of essays by U.S. opinion leaders from a range of professions who examined images of China from their respective vantage points. Although the two publications explore the same issue—the role of images in U.S.-China relations—from opposite sides, most notable are the similarities.

Among key findings of the earlier publication was that the U.S. self-image has influenced American perceptions of China perhaps more than any one action or set of actions on the part of the Chinese. In addition, U.S. images of China have gone through cycles of optimism and pessimism, the same sort of love-hate cycles that have characterized Chinese images of the United States. Similarly, those Americans who have had more contact with China were more likely to have positive images of China than those who had little or no contact.

As the chapters in this volume clearly demonstrate, where individual Chinese stand on the United States and the American people depends largely on where they sit. Those who have greater contact with Americans are more likely to form positive images of the United States, while those who are more isolated are left to form images based on American movies and Chinese propaganda. In the nineteenth and early twentieth centuries, traders and scholars like Sun Yat-sen presented a positive view of the United States. In contrast, Mao Zedong traveled outside China only twice, both times to the Soviet Union, and spent much of his time in power denouncing the United States. Today, according to a survey presented in this volume by Li Xiaogang in chapter eight, those who have worked or studied in the United States—returned overseas talents—feel more positively about Americans and the United States than do their counterparts who have not had the opportunity to interact regularly with Americans. Even the returned talents, however, differentiate between the American people and the U.S. government, and their feelings about the people are more positive than their feelings about the government.

Business executives hold mixed views, according to Ding Xinghao in chapter ten. They appreciate U.S. capital, technology, and expertise, but they find U.S. executives unpredictable and therefore risky to do business with. Chinese government officials, whose job it is to promote and protect the country's national interests, tend to be more distrustful than other Chinese of the United States, more "suspicious of U.S. hegemonic intentions," according to Gong Li in chapter three. Yet again, a dichotomy emerges: government officials often praise U.S. domestic policy, particularly its economic strength, but condemn U.S. foreign policy as unilateralist and arrogant. Chinese military and strategic experts are similarly wary of the United States. Moreover, according to Feng Changhong in chapter four, this group believes that the U.S. view of China as an economic and military competitor, or even a threat, has the potential to create a threat where one does not currently exist.

Most of the chapters that follow are written from the Chinese perspective, tracing the historical evolution of Chinese images of the United States and then looking at the views of specific Chinese constituency groups. Two U.S. scholars also weigh in on this critical topic. Terrill E. Lautz traces how U.S. perceptions of China, to a large degree shaped by self-image, have vacillated over time and have often been based on myth instead of reality. Derek J. Mitchell discusses how the proud U.S. self-image influences American views of China and how the gap between the way the United States sees itself and the way it is viewed by China and the world is a recipe for misunderstanding and miscalculation. From this volume, it is clear that the shaping of U.S.-China images and the bridging of the gap in perceptions will have a significant impact on how U.S.-China relations develop and, in turn, how the United States manages the emergence of China as a major player on the world stage.

Note

1. John Demos, "Viewpoints on the China Trade: A Young Nation Looks to the Pacific," *Common-place* 5, no. 2 (January 2005), www.common-place.org/vol-05/no-02/demos/index.shtml.

ACKNOWLEDGMENTS

THIS VOLUME is a compilation of papers that were written for an April 22, 2004, conference, "Chinese Images of the United States," which was hosted by the CSIS International Security Program (ISP) in cooperation with the Institute of American Studies at the Chinese Academy of Social Sciences (CASS) and the Center for American Studies at Fudan University. The conference was held at Fudan University in Shanghai. The conference was the second in a series of CSIS events focused on the role of images in U.S.-China relations; a conference, "China in the American Political Imagination," was held in Washington, D.C., on December 10, 2003, and a book of the same title was published in June 2003.

Kurt Campbell, CSIS senior vice president and ISP director, conceived of this project in conjunction with Christine Wing of the Ford Foundation in an effort to launch a dialogue on the critical issue of the impact of images on U.S. foreign policy making and U.S.-China relations. Derek J. Mitchell, ISP senior fellow, and Carola McGiffert, ISP fellow, developed the agenda and managed the project through completion. Ms. McGiffert wrote the preface and is also the principal editor of this publication. Kristine Schenck, ISP research assistant, organized the April event and oversaw the publication process. ISP interns Cynthia Carras, Brian Harding, and Sijin Chen also helped with the publication.

CSIS would like to thank Wang Jisi and Zhao Mei of CASS and Ni Shixiong and Sun Zhe of Fudan, as well as their colleagues and staff.

Without their intellectual guidance and hard work, this project would not have been possible, and we are deeply grateful for their support and partnership.

The conference and this publication were made possible by the generous support of the Henry Luce Foundation, the Ford Foundation, and Ronnie Chan of Hang Lung Properties Ltd. of Hong Kong. Conference speakers were selected to represent a wide range of perspectives, and the views expressed here are solely the responsibility of the authors.

PART ONE

EVOLUTION OF CHINESE PERCEPTIONS OF THE UNITED STATES

CHAPTER ONE

CHINESE IMAGES OF THE UNITED STATES
A HISTORICAL REVIEW

Hu Guocheng

THE U.S. MERCHANT SHIP *Empress of China* made the first direct Sino-American contact on a speculative voyage from New York to Guang-zhou—then under the rule of the Qianlong emperor—in 1784, during the Qing dynasty. The venture was a success, returning a 30 percent profit on an investment of $120,000,[1] encouraging ongoing trade between the two countries. Records of the Chinese customs agency show that between 1785 and 1838, 4,519 foreign merchant ships came to China to trade—and more than a one-quarter (1,150) were American. China was the fourth-largest trading partner of the United States in the first half of nineteenth century.[2]

With trade flourishing, cultural contacts between China and the United States began to expand. In 1830, the American Board of Commissioners for Foreign Missions, subsidized by American traders, sent the first American missionary, Elijah C. Bridgman, to China. By 1839, six other missionaries had joined him, and by 1850, the American missionary community had grown to 88 people. In addition to providing religious services in China, they also offered medical, educational, and publishing services. In fact, their writing and publishing had significantly more influence than did their traditional missionary work, and it contributed valuably to the mutual understanding between the two peoples.

Chinese Repository, an English-language periodical published from 1832 to 1851 and edited by Elijah Bridgman and Samuel Wells Williams, a well-known Congregational layman who arrived in Canton in 1833 as a printer for the American Board of Commissioners for Foreign Missions, offered Americans a unique window on Chinese politics, economics, history, and religion. *A Brief Guide to the United States of America*, a Chinese-language account written by Bridgman and published in Singapore in 1838, became one of the key sources at the time for Chinese intellectuals and officials who were learning about the United States.

Although no official diplomatic relations existed between China and the United States at that time, bilateral nongovernmental trade and people-to-people exchange flourished on the basis of mutual economic benefit and political equality. Commercial disputes occurred and criminal cases, such as opium smuggling by some U.S. businessmen, were brought, but the trend was toward increasingly close ties.

As a result, Chinese images of the United States were generally positive. Pioneers such as Wei Yuan and Xu Jiyu of the "open eyes to watch the world" generation and ordinary Chinese like Xie Qinggao who happened to visit the United States highly praised and admired the new country—its democratic system, its economic and technological development, and even its president, George Washington. In his 50 volumes of *Illustrated Gazetteer of the Countries Overseas,* Wei Yuan said that the United States "is rich and strong, brings no humiliation upon small countries, shows no contempt for China, and always champions those in distress. It is friendly, isn't it?"[3] A memorial tablet with an engraving written by Xu Jiyu praising George Washington is at the Washington Monument in Washington, D.C.

In 1844, China and the United States signed the Wangxia Treaty, which established official diplomatic relations between the two countries. The treaty promoted trade between China and the United States by granting Americans access to four new ports, lowering tariffs on U.S. goods, and giving extraterritorial rights to the United States. The treaty was viewed as not only unequal on trade terms but also a violation of China's sovereignty.

That official Sino-American relations were based on an unequal treaty cast a shadow on the relationship from the outset. During the Opium War (1839–1842), China fought against Great Britain, but the

United States seized the opportunity to follow the British gunboats, plundering Chinese interests and violating China's sovereignty. U.S. behavior in the Opium War sent a message to the Chinese that they must be vigilant against the United States.

In the early 1860s, Qing troops, aided by the American, Frederick T. Ward, and his foreign Shanghai rifle corps, fought to quash the Taiping Rebellion. During the Boxer movement, the United States Army helped suppress another rebellion, after which it forced the Chinese government to sign the Boxer Protocol. Both the Chinese people and the government began to view the United States as just another imperial power that sought to carve up China.

The U.S. Open Door policy and the return of part of the Boxer indemnity made a favorable impression on some Chinese, but, on balance, the United States in general and U.S. foreign policy in particular have been viewed with distrust since Wangxia. Even Li Hongzhang, the Chinese prime minister in the late Qing dynasty who is viewed as a traitor in China, said that while the United States "does not damage China, it does not benefit China." Sheng Xuanhuai, a provincial governor in the Qing government who shared Li's view, said that although the United States "does not want our territory, . . . it does absolutely not help us." After negotiating a commercial agreement with a U.S. delegation, Sheng pointed out that "the Americans show their kindness and say that they don't want to violate China's sovereignty, but they do their best to get their interests in China and to prevent from any loss and damage."[4]

It was the Chinese Exclusion Act of 1882 that most seriously damaged the relationship between China and the United States and led to a boycott of U.S. goods in 1905. During this period, Chinese images of the United States deteriorated. Chinese newspapers and magazines published numerous editorials and articles condemning the U.S. persecution of Chinese compatriots in the United States and exposing the hypocrisy of the U.S. government. An article published in *Fujian Everyday News* stated, "Enforcing power politics, despising truth, staining humanity, damaging relations between the two countries, these are humiliation upon 400 million people of China." *Lingdong Daily*, published in Guangdong province, pointed out that "throughout the country, all of the Chinese people think that the United States is playing a leading role in violating and damaging China."[5] In short, the U.S. exclusion policy toward China almost destroyed any lingering positive image of the United States in China.

Sun Yat-sen and his fellow revolutionaries sought to learn from the United States in their quest to establish a republic and make China rich and strong. After 1911, when the Republic of China (ROC) was established, Sun's positive views about the United States had an effect on the Chinese people, but it was short-lived.

After the end of World War I, Chinese people placed great hope on the Paris peace conference. Chinese people thought that victory in the war proved that "truth triumphs over power," and they hoped the conference would bring dignity and fairness to China as part of the victorious coalition. The Fourteen Points, initiated by President Woodrow Wilson, were welcomed by China. Chen Duxiu, one of the founders of the Chinese Communist Party, wrote an article in which he praised President Wilson as "the first good man in the world." However, the results of the conference shattered this illusion. Instead of giving back land to China, the land was merely redistributed. The German privilege in Shandong province was turned over to Japan, for example. Disappointment and anger led to the May 4th Movement—a patriotic movement initiated by students at Peking University and joined by workers in many Chinese cities. Even Chen Duxiu changed his tone: "What truth, what permanent peace, what President Wilson's Fourteen Points, all of these are totally worthless vain words!"[6]

By the time the Washington peace conference was held in 1921, most Chinese had a negative view of the United States. Once again, Chen Duxiu warned against false friends: "Don't be cheated by the U.S. imperialists," and "Don't lead a part of the people or young students to be friendly with the U.S. imperialism unconsciously."[7] In December 1923, a poll of Peking University students showed that less than 13 percent viewed the United States as a friend. In contrast, 59 percent viewed the Soviet Union as a friend.

Even Sun Yat-sen changed his view. Sun turned away from his former teacher, the United States, and looked to the Soviet Union. He began to argue that, because imperialist powers and Chinese warlords acted in collusion with each other, chaos in China was in fact controlled and supported by the outside powers and that "the United States must be especially responsible for it." He asked, "Has George Washington's and Abraham Lincoln's motherland thrown away her great faith for freedom, changing from a liberator into an oppressor who suppresses the people fighting for freedom?"[8]

Of course, there were still many Chinese who continued to have faith in America, including those Chinese studying in the United States. They admired U.S. democracy, science, and technology, which outweighed, in their minds, the negative issues associated with U.S. power politics. However, the influence of this group over Chinese society was shrinking.

During the war of resistance against Japanese aggression, Chinese images of the United States improved again because Chinese and Americans were fighting together against a common enemy, Japanese militarism. At that time, the U.S. government adopted a relatively balanced policy toward both the Chinese Communist Party (CCP) and the Kuomintang (KMT). It provided the KMT government with military and logistical supplies; sent an U.S. Army military observer group to Yan'an, the capital of the CCP base areas; and even sent the United States Air Force to join in the anti-Japanese battles. Attacks on Japanese communication lines by the famous Flying Tigers, or the 14th Air Force, and the brave Hump airlift by the U.S. Air Force in the China-Burma-India theater won great admiration and respect for the United States among the Chinese public. Chinese villagers risked their lives to rescue U.S. pilots from fighters that had crashed or were shot down by the Japanese. When President Franklin D. Roosevelt died in 1945, *Liberation Daily* and *New China Daily,* both published by the CCP in Yan'an, published editorials praising the U.S. president as "the banner of democracy" and "a giant star of democracy." Unfortunately, these positive images did not last long.

In the Liberation War (the Chinese civil war), the U.S. government supported KMT leader Chiang Kai-shek, who launched a war against the will of the people and the Chinese national government, which had lost popular credibility. As a result, Chinese images of the United States once again turned more negative. After the People's Republic of China (PRC) was established, the U.S. government's hostile policies toward new China recast the United States as an enemy in the minds of many Chinese.

Throughout history, Chinese images of the United States have shifted in concert with U.S. policy toward China. If U.S. government officials would consider the interests of other countries as they develop policy, images of the United States in China and around the world would be significantly improved.

Notes

1. Michael H. Hunt, *The Making of a Special Relationship: The United States and China to 1914* (New York: Columbia University Press, 1983), p. 2.

2. Tao Wenzhao, *The History of the Sino-American Relationship: 1911–1950* (Chongqing: Chongqing Press, 1993), pp. 3–4.

3. Quoted from Yang Yusheng, *Chinese Images of the U.S.* (Shanghai: Fudan University Press, 1997), pp. 12–13.

4. Xia Dongyuan, *A Sheng Xuanhuai Biography* (Chengdu: Sichuan People's Press, 1988), p. 339.

5. Quoted from Yang, *Chinese Images of the U.S.,* pp. 38–39.

6. Chen Duxiu, *Selected Works of Chen Duxiu,* vol. 1 (Shanghai: Shanghai People's Publishing House, 1993), pp. 304, 397.

7. Chen Duxiu, *Selected Works of Chen Duxiu,* vol. 2 (Shanghai: Shanghai People's Publishing House, 1993), p. 214.

8. Quoted from Yang, *Chinese Images of the U.S.,* p. 72.

CHAPTER TWO

FROM PAPER TIGER TO REAL LEVIATHAN

CHINA'S IMAGES OF THE UNITED STATES SINCE 1949

Wang Jisi

AFTER THE COMMUNIST PARTY TOOK POWER in China in 1949, the Chinese leadership identified itself as a staunch ally of the Soviet Union in ideological, political, military, and economic terms and regarded the United States as the archenemy of China. As a result, China's perceptions of the United States shifted drastically to the negative.

HISTORICAL CONTRAST

The image of the United States was particularly dramatized by the U.S.-China confrontation during the Korean War in 1950–1953. On October 26, 1950, one day after the formal entrance of the PRC in the Korean War, the central leadership of the CCP internally circulated a document instructing the party to conduct anti-U.S. propaganda.[1]

This document was probably the first authorized attempt to systematically shape the image of the United States in China. It called for a "unified understanding and position on U.S. imperialism" and a thorough, resolute political campaign to "wipe out the pro-American reactionary thoughts and the American-phobia psychology, and to foster a widespread attitude of hating, disdaining, and despising the United States."

The document described the United States in three images. First, eight historical events were listed to illustrate that the United States was the Chinese nation's enemy. Second, three reasons were given to explain why the United States was also an enemy of the whole world: the United States (1) was the headquarters of launching wars of international aggression, and it made profits by killing people with advanced weapons; (2) was the headquarters of opposing democracy and fostering fascism in other parts of the world; and (3) was an enemy of civilization and the headquarters of human spiritual degeneration. Finally, the document depicted the United States as a "paper tiger." According to the propaganda line it prescribed, Americans were not only politically isolated but also militarily weakened by overstretching, and they were no longer monopolizing the atom bomb.

It was not this document but the Communist leader Mao Zedong who first created the paper-tiger analogy in 1946 when he was interviewed by the American correspondent, Anna Louise Strong. Mao commented in the interview:

> Chiang Kai-shek and his supporters, the U.S. reactionaries, are all paper tigers too. Speaking of U.S. imperialism, people seem to feel that it is terrifically strong. Chinese reactionaries are using the "strength" of the United States to frighten the Chinese people. But it will be proved that the U.S. reactionaries, like all the reactionaries in history, do not have much strength.[2]

The defeat of Chiang Kai-shek proved to the Chinese Communists that he and his U.S. supporters were indeed paper tigers. This view was reinforced by the result of the Korean War, in which China claimed victory over the world's most powerful imperialist country, one armed with nuclear weapons. During and after the Korean War, the accusation of tendencies in China of *qinmei* (pro-American) and *kongmei* (American-phobia) became a customary propaganda effort, and *fanmei* (anti-American) feelings were officially stimulated.

In the 1950s and 1960s, the United States attempted to isolate the PRC politically and economically and contain it militarily, and it sent its troops to protect Taiwan from any Chinese effort to take the island to achieve national reunification. The image of the United States as the archenemy of China and of the whole world was consolidated. Meanwhile, China saw the U.S. paper tiger as deeply wounded by international revolutions and by the erosion of capitalism. The Vietnam War, the Cuban revolution, and a number of other setbacks in the U.S. conflict with the Soviet Union as well as in the Third World undermined its strength. The U.S. civil rights movement in the 1960s, especially the vehement struggle represented by Martin Luther King Jr., presented an image to the Chinese that the paper tiger was suffering from serious problems at home.

In addition to viewing the United States as China's primary security threat, the Chinese people were being educated to believe that the United States was the most sinister Western power and was trying to corrode Chinese culture and national identity by spreading decadent bourgeois ideas and lifestyles. Such efforts before 1949 were exemplified by American missionary activities, the Open Door policy, and the refunding of part of the Boxer indemnity to establish Western schools and hospitals in China and bring Chinese students to the United States for training. John Foster Dulles, secretary of state in the Eisenhower administration, made himself known to every Chinese with political consciousness by making a statement in June 1957 that his government should do everything possible to contribute to the end of the Communist rule in China.[3] Therefore, the United States was also seen as a real, ferocious, but hypocritical tiger capable of threatening China's political and cultural survival. During the Cultural Revolution, a number of political figures (such as the wife of State Chairman Liu Shaoqi) and intellectuals were accused of being U.S. agents or followers. Virtually nothing related to the United States was perceived as positive.

The rapprochement between the two countries in the early 1970s gradually brought about a new U.S. image in China. The Soviet Union, called the "new czar" of "social imperialism," eclipsed the United States as the most dangerous threat to China's national security and domestic stability. An apparently weakened United States was described as defensive in international politics, playing the role as a counterweight to Soviet expansion. However, the Chinese lament of the decline of U.S. power was confined to geopolitical calculations in facing the Soviet threat. The U.S. role in world affairs, particularly in world economics, continued to be seen as negative.

After China entered the reform era in 1979, a year also marked by the establishment of China-U.S. diplomatic relations, positive elements were found in America's image in China. Although the official line continued to call for vigilance against U.S. political and cultural penetration, Chinese students and the intelligentsia at large became quite enthusiastic about U.S. politics, culture, education, and society. Some were obviously inspired by America's liberal democratic ideas in promulgating their own proposals for reforming China. In the 1980s, especially between 1986 and 1989, owing to a combination of factors, the positive part of America's image culminated among the Chinese population. Among those factors were the official denunciation of the Cultural Revolution under Mao Zedong, the Sino-U.S. strategic coordination against the Soviet bloc (including tacit U.S. support for China's border war with Vietnam), an unprecedented aspiration for opening and reform, the burgeoning market economy, and the emphasis on higher education and scientific research.

This contrast of images was dramatically sharpened by the 1989 Tiananmen turmoil, during which a number of student demonstrators, while listening to a Voice of America broadcast expressing support for them, believed they were representing contemporary Chinese democratization. Indeed, relaxation of East-West relations, *glasnost* in the Soviet Union, and political upheavals in Eastern Europe seemed to have convinced the student activists and their sympathizers that Western-type democracy was the tide of the day. However, the Tiananmen movement soon ended with a resolute crackdown, followed by a more vigorous authorized effort to reintroduce the traditional political education about the harmfulness of U.S. thinking and "conspiratorial schemes" about China.

The 1990s witnessed some interesting flip-flops in Chinese perceptions of the United States, reflecting the ups and downs in the U.S.-China relationship throughout history. Growing commercial ties led to U.S. products—including Hollywood movies and McDonald's—becoming exceedingly popular among Chinese citizens. The zeal for studying and working in the United States only grew. This positive image reached its peak in 1997–1998 when President Jiang Zemin and President Bill Clinton exchanged official visits and stated their shared interest in "building toward a constructive strategic partnership" between the two countries.

At the same time, during the 1990s the image of the United States was tainted by a number of events as well as U.S. actions abroad. The annual debate in the U.S. Congress over whether to grant China most-favored-nation (MFN) trade status, the Clinton administration's decision to issue a visa to Taiwan's Lee Teng-hui in 1995, continued U.S. arms sales to Taiwan, and Washington's human rights pressures on Beijing were often referred to as indications of U.S. hostility toward a country that harbored no antagonistic intentions. To this extent, the Chinese government was successful in convincing its citizens that the United States was a sinister hegemon trying to dominate the world and interfere in China's domestic affairs. According to China's official guideline, U.S. policy toward China aimed to Westernize (*xihua*), divide (*fenhua*), and contain (*ezhi*) the People's Republic with ulterior motives.

Chinese disillusionment with the United States was coupled with impressive economic performance and social progress in China. Beijing claimed that China's achievements were due largely to political stability at home and resistance to U.S. calls for freedom of speech and democracy. Radical nationalistic feelings were vented by a controversial but popular book, *China Can Say No,* published in 1996. The accumulated agony about U.S. hegemonic behavior in world affairs soared in May 1999 after U.S. bombs hit the Chinese embassy in Belgrade and killed three Chinese reporters. The embassy bombing once again evoked the collective memories of China's one hundred years of humiliation after the Opium War. The trauma was so deep that the vast majority of Chinese elites still believe today that the bombing was intentional, not a "mistake" as the U.S. government claimed. Any random interviews with Chinese citizens would affirm this conclusion.

Since 2000, the Chinese public has generally held a more balanced and stable view of the United States than in the past. In the global power equation, the United States seems to loom even larger in Chinese overall strategic thinking, as post–September 11 America has been more aggressive in taking military actions and as the U.S. economy continues to have an edge over European and Japanese economies. On the other hand, Beijing's official pronouncements have played down the themes of "multipolarity" and "opposing hegemony" and have described Beijing's relationship with Washington as correctly improving. Generally,

Chinese media have reported U.S. domestic and foreign affairs in more detached and objective terms.

The air collision between a Chinese fighter plane and a U.S. spy plane, known as EP-3, over the island of Hainan in April 2001 triggered a political crisis in China-U.S. relations. During this period of crisis, the "enemy image" of the United States resurfaced, although the public reaction to the EP-3 incident was less emotional than the reaction to the Belgrade embassy bombing in 1999, largely owing to the more measured government handling of the incident.

The September 11, 2001, tragedy came five months after the EP-3 crisis, just as the U.S.-China relationship was returning to normal. China's leadership wasted no time in sending sympathies and condolences to the Bush administration, taking this opportunity to improve its image in the United States. Beijing also extended various forms of important but largely unreported support, including intelligence sharing, to the U.S. combat against terrorism in Afghanistan and elsewhere. In contrast, the general public in China harbored mixed feelings toward the 9/11 attacks. Some people were genuinely sympathetic with Americans, others got excited to see the dramatically shocking video pictures, and still others did not hide their pleasure in watching Americans suffer from, in their view, much deserved "punishment." The divergent reactions to 9/11 among Chinese citizens can be attributed to many factors. Notably, the apparently restrained Chinese media coverage of the tragic event did not fully report on sacrifices of Americans, moving stories about the rescue workers, or the mourning ceremonies.

Chinese perceptions of the United States became even more diversified when massive demonstrations occurred around the world in the spring of 2003 against an imminent U.S. war against Iraq. At that time, Beijing was trying to remain disengaged from the Iraq controversy. Since early 2002, China's official media had conspicuously refrained from castigating "U.S. hegemony," which was featured in the Chinese press for years in the 1990s.

Under the surface, however, China's political and intellectual elites debated heatedly about U.S. behavior in waging the war in Iraq. On one end of the debate, more than 400 intellectuals, retired officials, and Chinese overseas signed an emotional statement—which they distributed on the Internet—against America's "flagrant aggression." They accused the United States of being "a country that owns the largest amount of destructive weapons, a country that used to slaughter other nations and peoples with weapons of mass destruction, and a country that is always raising a butcher's knife and has never stopped killing and looting." "Is there any justification," they asked in the statement, "for that country to impose weapons inspection and make the most inhuman military attacks on a nation and a people (Iraq) that dares to resist its rude and unreasonable savage act?"[4]

At the other extreme, some Chinese thinkers were firmly convinced that the United State was morally justified and highly principled in its campaign to topple Saddam Hussein and to "liberate the Iraqi people." In their eyes, the confrontation between the United States and Iraq was one of "democratic values against dictatorship." One cynical commentator pointed out in an Internet chat room that certain arguments of this wing of thinking were "more pro-American than Americans themselves."

Such a gulf of opinion was never reflected in China's making of foreign policy. The Chinese leadership seemed unperturbed in viewing the United States pragmatically as the only global superpower with which China must manage to strengthen ties, particularly economic cooperation. Meanwhile, the official view remained that China should say no to U.S. exhortation of democracy and human rights because these U.S. schemes would impinge upon China's sovereignty and subordinate China to U.S. hegemonic domination of the world.

CONTEXTUAL CONTRAST

Along with the noticeable decrease in ideological indoctrination in China in the reform era, there has been little deliberate effort on the part of the Communist Party to shape the U.S. image in Chinese society, as was done in the 1950s–1970s. To be sure, the official line continues to point to the United States as the mainstay of the "hostile forces" that try to destabilize China and refers to the United States as the hegemonic power that threatens global security. However, it is up to individual observers to shape up their ideas regarding the U.S. economy, society, culture, politics, and foreign policy. It is encouraging that a substantially revised history textbook, in which descriptions of the United States are admiringly objective, has been adopted in China as of autumn 2004.[5] A new generation of educators, researchers, and analysts—many of whom studied in the United States or other countries and have been more exposed to a diverse range of views of the United States–is now assuming important government positions. This bodes well for more pluralistic observations of the United States.

In Chinese history since 1949, several images of the United States can be identified: a paper tiger that would be defeated by the Soviet Union, China, Vietnam, Cuba, or other revolutionary, anti-imperialist forces around the world; a superpower at par with the Soviet Union that could serve as a counterweight to the Soviet threat to Chinese security; the only hegemonic power that threatens world peace and stability in the post–Cold War era; an opponent to the rise of China that violates China's territorial integrity and prevents it from achieving national reunification; an economic engine that drives the world economy and, to an increasing extent, the Chinese economy; an admirable society that boasts having the most advanced scientific and technological know-how and the best educational system; a model of modernization from which China has a lot to learn; and an ideologically driven power that wants to influence China's political destiny. Different parts and layers of Chinese society may look at the United States through their own prisms and see different dimensions of that nation.

Strategic and Security Dimension

The first dimension is the strategic and security dimension, in which the United States is a Leviathan in Chinese eyes today. Some sophisticated strategists, diplomats, and international relations specialists see some value in the U.S. role in international affairs as a stabilizer and a balancer.

This understanding has an impact on Beijing's strategic thinking as recorded in China's official statement that it welcomes the "positive role" of the United States in East Asia. Most of the time and probably to most Chinese observers, however, the United States is an insatiable, domineering country that believes only in its own absolute power, one that would never allow any other country to catch up with it. Some of these Chinese may want to call the United States a "rogue empire," while others are less emotional but nonetheless puzzled by the U.S. habit of "putting its fingers in every pie" in global affairs.

One frequently raised question in recent years is: why does a domestically democratic nation act in such an undemocratic way in world affairs? Chinese refer to the unilateralist tendencies in the Bush administration's diplomacy, the U.S. propensity to resort to the use of force in settling international disputes, and the apparent arrogance in U.S. attitudes toward other nations. In particular, they see little legitimacy for the Bush administration to launch a war against Iraq in opposition to the opinion of the obvious majority of international society, including many traditional U.S. allies. The increased aggressiveness in U.S. foreign policy today has added to Chinese disillusionment about the United States being a benign superpower.

Without any doubt, the single most important issue that arouses Chinese indignation about the "hegemonic behavior" of the United States has been its policy toward Taiwan. Few, if any, Chinese on the mainland doubt that Taiwan is a Chinese territory and that people in Taiwan belong to the same Chinese nation as mainlanders. Therefore, the U.S. rejection of China's territorial claim of Taiwan and its continued arms sales to the island as part of the plans to thwart Chinese efforts to reunify it are regarded as showing hostility to the Chinese nation. One remarkably popular view is that the U.S. commitment to the defense of Taiwan is aimed at preventing China from becoming a unified nation that is rising up as a great power in the world.

Socioeconomic and Cultural Dimension

The second dimension is the socioeconomic and cultural dimension, in which the United States is generally regarded as a vanguard. Businesspeople, educators, students, scientists, technicians, and people of other professional backgrounds tend to be immensely impressed with the U.S. economic performance, standard of living, technological prowess, educational levels, and cultural product. Regardless of their political judgment of the external behavior of the United States, they do not hesitate to visit that remote foreign land. In this regard, the vast majority of these people do want China to be more like the United States.

One telling example of Chinese seeing the United States as a vanguard, which is certainly not peculiar to China, is the unswerving desire of students and professionals to seek training in the United States. A great many Chinese parents and grandparents, including those who hold strong anti-American political views, do not conceal their pride in having their children or grandchildren study in the United States. They eagerly tell people that their children or grandchildren have become U.S. citizens or are holding a green card. Chinese in China who express favorable views of the United States are often accused of being pro-American, unpatriotic, disloyal to China, or of being traitors; but Chinese who have opportunities to live in the United States or have obtained U.S. citizenship are often admired in Chinese society.

Political and Ideological Dimension

The third dimension is the political and ideological dimension, where America's image is split into a variety of faces. The mainstream official thinking in China that is presented, as well as represented, by ideological and propaganda institutions depicts the United States as a powerful infiltrator and meddler that interferes—with ulterior motives—in China's domestic affairs. This image of a U.S. threat is most often propagated by those organizations that are responsible for maintaining China's internal order or carrying out religious policy. Outside of those political circles, however, it is not a very widely held point of view because the U.S. role as a troublemaker in Chinese domestic political affairs is not really relevant to the daily life of the general public. It is undeniable that the image of the United States as a "beacon of freedom" does exist in the Chinese intelligentsia; however, such a reference is rarely heard outside of a small number of intellectual and political dissident groups.

One may argue that these images of the United States are contradictory. However, it is not difficult to imagine that they coexist in the Chinese heart, depending on the context and the moment in history. A typical Chinese intellectual or professional between the ages of 40 and 50 may be quite critical of U.S. international behavior, expecting more setbacks in the U.S. occupation of Iraq and hoping to see stronger counterweights, such as Russia and Europe, to U.S. power in the international arena. That same person, however, is not particularly interested in world politics as it is too remote from daily life. What may be more attractive to this person are things that can symbolize the U.S. lifestyle or their own American dream: a laptop computer (IBM), a personal car (a Buick), a big apartment, more hi-tech products, a freer working environment, or an opportunity to tour the United States. Memories of Tiananmen in 1989 have faded; gone with them is the image of the Statue of Liberty. The United States may be distinctively impressive for the way the country runs its own politics and society, but China has such a long and entrenched tradition that America's experiences can only be selectively and gradually borrowed, not totally adapted. Will China become more like the United States when China follows its own path of development? Most might privately, although reluctantly, answer yes.

AMERICAN IMAGE OR CHINA'S MIRROR IMAGE?

China's image of the United States is to a great extent its mirror image and reflects its own national aspirations, identity, traits, and culture. In fact, changing China's images of the United States is more the result of changing Chinese realities than changing U.S. realities.

In China's modern history, the United States has always served as its reference for modernity, nation building, and great-power status. Chinese gradualist reformers like Kang Youwei and Liang Qichao, liberal-minded intellectuals like Hu Shi, and revolutionary leaders like Sun Yat-sen and Mao Zedong all used to express their respect for America's national experiences and experimentation. And all of them used to praise American political institutions and showed a strong desire to learn from them.

Meanwhile, the Russian revolution in 1917 and the triumph of the Soviet Union in achieving industrialization and great-power status caused Chinese Communists and their sympathizers to view the Soviet Union as an alternative model of modernization. After 1949, the PRC made painstaking efforts to follow the Soviet model until Chinese leaders clashed with and were disillusioned by the Soviets in the 1960s. However, the departure from the Stalinist model since then has not been, and is not meant to be, a completed process. Although the collapse of the Soviet Union dealt a heavy blow to those Chinese who harbored nostalgic feelings about the Soviet model, apprehensions about the possible downfall of Chinese socialism prevented Chinese leaders from denying the values of Soviet experiences and from looking at the United States as an alternative.

Thus, perceptions of the United States, especially the expressed views of its values, political ideas, institutions, and international strategy, are politically very sensitive because a value judgment of the United States may well be interpreted as a value judgment of China itself. In many cases, it is indeed a value judgment about where China should be heading. For example, criticisms of the U.S. presidential elections for being influenced by money imply that China should not introduce such democratic mechanisms. By the same token, censure of the U.S.-led North Atlantic Treaty Organization (NATO) military operations in Kosovo as "humanitarian intervention" served the purpose of guarding against possible U.S. intervention in China under similar circumstances. In another example—this in a positive sense—advocates for China's gigantic plans for developing its automobile industry often refer to the fact that, on average, most U.S. households own more than one car.

Understanding of the United States by the Chinese people is by necessity subject to their own cultural interpretation. For example, Chinese rejection of the U.S. claim to a leadership role in global affairs is based partly on Chinese definitions of leaders and their qualifications. To the Chinese, leadership, or *lingdao,* must be essentially a hierarchical order, a superior-inferior relationship. Therefore, to the Chinese, because the most important principle in the world of nations is national sovereignty and international equality and because China is one of the greatest civilizations and the most populous country in the world, China cannot be led by the United States or be subordinated to it.

It is also self-evident in Chinese culture that a good ruler or leader must be a moral example, showing conscience and benevolence for the people rather than putting personal interests before the interests of the citizens. However, in Chinese eyes, external U.S. behavior is driven by its own interests, not the interests of the other countries it wants to lead. Moreover, Americans unscrupulously admit it! The tradition of justifying one's behavior by showing good intentions and selflessness puts those Chinese who want to defend U.S. foreign policy in an embarrassing position because they are hardly able to present a United States that works to serve the interests of other nations.

To most Chinese observers, American people are characteristically pragmatic and driven by personal interest, as portrayed in Hollywood movies and witnessed in personal encounters. Also very pragmatic, Chinese people find it difficult to imagine and comprehend Americans' adherence to their basic values in general and their religious faith in particular. To be sure, the Chinese people used to adore Mao Zedong almost as a living god and regard Mao Zedong's thoughts as a faith, but Chinese society is mostly atheist. The personal cult for Mao is seen today as an aberration and an anachronism. Since the end of the Cultural Revolution, Chinese people have overcome the ideological fervor that marked that era and have become increasingly materialistic.

To many Chinese, young and old, ideology and religion are nothing but a disguise to cover up material interests, instruments to achieve particular economic or political goals. As a result, they are skeptical of U.S. concerns about human rights in other countries and tend to think these concerns are simply a policy instrument to serve other policy goals. In the Chinese imagination, Americans believe in social Darwinism and the law of the jungle. As such, the foreign policy of the Bush administration, galvanized by Americans' interest in dominating the world and guided by "hard realism" or "offensive realism," reveals the true colors of the United States.

The disparity between the two nations' social institutions also results in Chinese misperceptions. The Chinese polity has always been hierarchically organized, and government intervention is omnipresent. Civil society remains an alien notion. It is not easy for an ordinary Chinese to imagine that a city mayor in the United States may not take orders from a state governor, and a state governor may not follow the instructions from a U.S. president. Neither is it easy to understand how a nongovernmental organization (NGO) can work abroad on its own without being supported by the government. Ordinary Chinese believe an "invisible hand," be it the Central Intelligence Agency (CIA) or other U.S. government agency, gives directions and coordinates NGO programs abroad. Thus, conspiracy theories are particularly popular among Chinese in explaining U.S. international behavior.

Chinese perceptions of the United States are primarily developed by China's own conditions and experiences and less so by transformations in U.S. society, politics, and foreign policy. Nonetheless, a stable and fruitful U.S.-China relationship and a better U.S. understanding of China will naturally help reconstruct U.S. images in China in a more positive way.

Notes

1. "Zhonggong Zhongyang Guanyu Zai Quanguo Jinxing Shishi Xuanchuan De Zhishi" [Instructions of the CPC Central Committee on the nationwide propaganda about the current events], October 26, 1950; reprinted in *Jianguo Yilai Zhongyao Wenxian Xuanbian* [Selection of important documents since the foundation of the PRC], vol. 1 (Beijing: Central Documentation Press, 1992), pp. 436–448.

2. "Talk with the American Correspondent Anna Louise Strong, August 1946," *Selected Works of Mao Tse-tung,* vol. 4 (Beijing: Foreign Languages Press, 1975), p. 101.

3. "Dulles's speech on China policy to the Lions International, San Francisco, June 28, 1957," reprinted in *Sino-American Relations, 1949–71,* documented and introduced by Roderick MacFarquhar (New York: Praeger, 1972), pp. 134–142.

4. "Zhongguo Xuezhe Lianming Fanzhan" [Chinese scholars sign up to oppose the Iraq war], *21 Shiji Huanqiu Baodao* [Global tribune of the twenty-first century], February 17, 2003.

5. Chen Wutong and Li Weike, eds., *History* (senior high school textbook), book 2 (Beijing: People's Education Press, 2004), especially unit 6, pp. 118–133.

PART TWO

ELITE VIEWS OF THE UNITED STATES

CHAPTER THREE
_____

THE OFFICIAL PERSPECTIVE
WHAT CHINESE GOVERNMENT OFFICIALS THINK OF AMERICA

Gong Li

THE QUALITY OF CHINESE GOVERNMENT OFFICIALS has improved significantly over the past decades. Today, most officials are well educated. After entrance examinations were resumed, those planning to enter the government were able to attend and graduate from college, and many have graduate degrees. As a result, their field of vision tends to be comparatively wider than that of their predecessors, and they are conscious that, in the era of economic globalization, China's development is inseparable from the world. The United States, as the world's most powerful and advanced nation, will inevitably have great influence on modernization in China. Therefore, most Chinese government officials pay great attention to the U.S. experience of rapid growth and development of a market economy and its foreign policy, especially toward China.

Many Chinese government officials have visited, conducted research, and even studied in the United States. Some have received U.S. visitors to China. As a result, they have had the experience of observing at close range the United States and its people. They also learn about the United States through television, radio, the Internet, and various newspapers and books. Many have children or relatives studying or working in the United States. In other words, in contrast with those in other professions or social strata, officials have a number of channels through which they can get to know the United States.

Compared with other Chinese, government officials attach more importance to safeguarding China's national interest in the development of Sino-U.S. relations, and they oppose U.S. intervention in China's domestic affairs. In addition, they are more ideological than their non-government counterparts; they seek to prevent China from becoming Westernized or divided and are concerned about U.S. influence on China's national security and economic modernization.

Of course, government officials' views of the United States have varied since the founding of the PRC. From 1949 to the end of the 1950s, government officials viewed the United States through an ideological lens. At that time, most government officials were veterans of both the war against Japanese aggression and the war against Chiang Kai-shek. U.S. support for Chiang and the Nationalists was fresh in their memories, and they generally held negative views about both the U.S. domestic system and its foreign policy. After the Korean War broke out and the U.S. Seventh Fleet entered the Taiwan Strait, Chinese government officials became more worried about the U.S. threat to China's security. Generally speaking, at that time, officials saw the United States as China's most dangerous enemy. After the cease-fire in Korea, Chinese government officials continued to hold hostile and suspicious attitudes toward the United States owing to Sino-U.S. diplomatic friction and the deadlock over the Taiwan problem. Later, Secretary of State John Foster Dulles spoke about bringing about peaceful evolution in socialist countries; Chinese government officials paid close attention.

In the 1960s, interference by the United States in the Vietnam War was regarded by Chinese government officials as an effort to pressure or threaten China from another strategic direction. Because of the split between China and the Soviet Union, the United States was no longer the only big state that China needed to oppose. In the latter part of the decade, based in part on historical relations between China and Russia, Chinese hostility toward the Soviet Union exceeded its hostility toward the United States. Sino-Soviet confrontation increased, as seen in the armed incident on Zhenbao Island on the Sino-Soviet border, and Chinese government officials began to regard the Soviet Union as China's greatest security threat. As a result, tensions in the Sino-U.S. relationship relaxed and the process of Sino-U.S. rapprochement began.

In April 1971, China and the United States began to come closer as a result of the first visit to China by the U.S. Ping-Pong team, which in turn helped improve the image of the United States in Chinese eyes. The Chinese media also began to tone down its negative rhetoric against the United States and thereby helped reshape the image of the United States. Of course, Chinese government officials knew of the CCP Central Committee's new, more friendly policy toward the United States earlier than other Chinese citizens. At the June 1971 Central Working Conference, senior cadres came to understand Mao Zedong's strategy of relaxing tensions with the United States. Later, a transcript of Mao Zedong's talk with Edgar Snow, a U.S. correspondent, was passed down the party ranks to the grass roots.

The decision to ease Sino-U.S. tensions was resented by the Gang of Four but was accepted by most Chinese government officials without much difficulty, primarily because the historical image of the United States is better than that of Japan—in part because of U.S. support to China in its fight against Japanese aggression—and of Russia. Most significant in shaping government officials' perceptions of the United States was their assessment that the Soviets were adopting an aggressive attitude and the United States a defensive attitude in the Cold War, and that the U.S. threat to China would decrease over time while opportunities for better relations would increase. After President Richard Nixon's visit to China, Chinese government officials became even more interested in the United States, and the image of the United States became more and more positive. This does not mean that Chinese government officials approved of the American social system or American values. Instead, they sought to take advantage of the U.S.-Soviet confrontation to concentrate their efforts against the Soviet Union. There were simply more common interests between China and the United States than between China and the Soviet Union. Chinese government officials began to see Nixon, Henry Kissinger, and others who took part in opening the door of Sino-U.S. relations as friends.

In October 1976, a tremendous change took place on the Chinese political stage. Healthy forces in the CCP crushed the Gang of Four. The Cultural Revolution, which had lasted 10 years, came to an end. In 1978, at the initiative of Deng Xiaoping, the Chinese government made economic construction its top priority and set reform and an opening-up policy as its basis. These profound changes established a new dynamic in the normalization of Sino-U.S. relations. At the same time, the image of the United States underwent tremendous change in the eyes of China. The United States became the most important state in the West; from it, China could learn and gain access to advanced technologies and management.

Chinese government officials expected that improvement of Sino-U.S. relations would provide a beneficial international environment for domestic construction, reform, and opening. An improvement in relations would also contribute to the realization of the grand goal of modernization with the aid of U.S. capital, technology, and administrative expertise.

After the establishment of diplomatic relations between China and the United States, communication and cooperation between the two states developed in an unprecedented fashion. In the process, Chinese government officials had more opportunities than common people to visit and conduct research in the United States. As a result, they were able to increase their understanding of the United States. U.S. national power, advanced technology, and convenient communications impressed them greatly. Generally, they thought the United States could play an important role in helping China modernize.

Chinese government officials' impressions of the United States were most positive and least ideological during the 1980s. To be sure, a few officials continued to be suspicious of the United States, and tensions—such as over Taiwan, human rights, trade, and proliferation—remained in the Sino-U.S. relationship. But generally these problems did not fundamentally influence Chinese government officials' positive view of the United States because such problems were not considered mainstream and were limited by both sides to a certain area and degree.

After the Tiananmen incident in Beijing in 1989, the United States sanctioned China on the pretext of poor human rights. Then came sweeping changes in the Soviet Union and Eastern Europe. Chinese government officials felt that the situation had become dangerous and urgent. At that time, discussions took place in Chinese political circles that China should work to prevent the United States from Westernizing and dividing China, which in part reflects China's anger at U.S. criticism of its human rights record. Although most Chinese government officials did not like the United States exerting pressure on China, they understood that developing normal relations with the United States was in China's fundamental national interest. Therefore, when Deng Xiaoping suggested that "even though there are some troubles, problems and differences, the relations between China and America should become well eventually,"[1] most Chinese government officials agreed.

Sino-U.S. relations improved over the course of the 1990s, especially after President Jiang Zemin's visit to the United States in 1997 and President Bill Clinton's visit to China in 1998. This more positive trend was reversed by the U.S. bombing of the Chinese embassy in Belgrade in 1999 and the clash between Chinese and U.S. aircraft over the sea near Hainan Island in 2001. Chinese government officials reacted quite vehemently to both events. After these two incidents, Chinese government officials' dominant view was that the United States was pursuing a policy of hegemony. That said, compared with the Chinese masses, the attitude of Chinese government officials toward the United States was relatively restrained.

After 9/11, Sino-U.S. relations developed on the basis of antiterrorism cooperation. At this point, about one-third of Chinese government officials were optimistic about Sino-U.S. relations. This group maintained that common interests outweigh contradictions between China and the United States, and, therefore, if both sides handle the relationship properly, no sharp tensions would emerge. Another third thought that Sino-U.S. relations would continue to fluctuate as a result of the dual nature of U.S. policy toward China. Sino-U.S. relations would be marked by frequent twists and turns—periods of contact followed by periods of restraint and friction. This group nonetheless maintained that the relationship, if handled properly, would not go astray completely. The other third of government officials was skeptical about U.S. strategic intentions toward China. They suggested that the United States would not tolerate the emergence of a strong China that could become a threat to U.S. hegemonic status worldwide. Therefore, struggle and confrontation between the two countries was all but inevitable. Finally, a few felt that too many variables existed in the Sino-U.S. relationship to predict how it would develop in the future.

U.S. policy toward Taiwan has been the most problematic issue for Chinese government officials. In their view, America's Taiwan policy, including arms sales, is motivated by a desire to delay or even prevent China's rise. Alternatively, U.S. policy toward Taiwan is seen as an effort by the United States to use democratization in Taiwan to promote peaceful political evolution in mainland China. Some officials also suspect that the United States wants to turn Taiwan into an unsinkable U.S. aircraft carrier. Only a very small minority believes that U.S. policy toward Taiwan is designed to protect U.S. interests in the Asia-Pacific and live up to its international commitments, as the United States claims.

Concerns about U.S. efforts to contain China have spilled over into the commercial realm as well. Most Chinese government officials believe that trade tensions are related to a U.S. containment strategy, an effort to stop China's rise to power. A few even think that the United States is trying to change the Chinese political system through trade.

Chinese government officials tend to doubt and distrust U.S. intentions toward China. Take Taiwan again: Americans feel a commitment to Taiwan, but Chinese officials see Taiwan as a matter of the independence, sovereignty, territorial integrity, and national dignity of China. Most officials believe that any PRC government that yields on Taiwan would be considered traitorous. Since coming to power, Taiwan President Chen Shui-bian has insisted on "one country on each side" and has sought to draw up a constitution by referendum, causing continuous tensions across the Taiwan Strait. Chinese officials naturally associate constitutional efforts with their belief that the United States would intervene if there were a conflict in the strait, which in turn would lead to full confrontation between China and the United States. U.S. attacks on China's human rights, dictatorship, and autocracy also make Chinese government officials question whether the United States doubts Chinese sovereignty. Chinese officials are also alert to U.S. attempts to Westernize or divide China. This does not mean that Chinese government officials do not support reform of the political system and expansion of democracy in China. Most do, in fact, but they oppose political reform if it is solely an imitation of the U.S. model.

In addition, Chinese government officials have been disgusted by U.S. unilateralism in dealing with international problems. Regarding

Iraq, for example, a majority of Chinese government officials thought that, while it was reasonable to overthrow Saddam Hussein, it was not correct for the United States to take action outside the United Nations (UN). Some firmly opposed the war waged by the United States, and only a tiny minority supported U.S. action in Iraq. Many officials were worried that indiscriminate preemptive measures taken by the United States would set a precedent that could one day be directed at China.

In contrast with their views on U.S. foreign policy, Chinese government officials hold positive views about U.S. domestic affairs. For example, most think the U.S. democratic system and market economy have brought prosperity and stability to the United States. At the same time, they do not think that the U.S. model could be effectively applied to developing countries, especially China. Only about 15 percent of officials believe that the U.S. political system is of universal significance and worth studying and learning from. An even smaller minority believes that the U.S. political system is a bogus democracy that serves the interests of the rich only.

As China has become more open to the outside, Chinese government officials' views and impressions about the United States, compared with officials' views in the past, have changed a lot. The tendency today is to be more objective and practical. Few either fully embrace or fully reject the United States. Most appreciate U.S. cultural products such as literature, art, music, film, and television, although about one-quarter believe that U.S. culture is too commercial or in bad taste. Some are worried about an American cultural invasion, designed to propagandize American values. These people argue for limitations on U.S. cultural products into China.

Chinese government officials have a positive view of U.S. higher education and advanced technology. Most would like to send their children to the United States to study and even would not oppose having their children work in the United States after graduation. In fact, the number of officials whose children study or work in the United States is higher than the number from other social strata. Senior or midlevel officials who enjoy more privileges regularly send their children to study or work in United States; others are more dependent on scholarships because of limited economic resources.

Most officials welcome U.S. goods and capital into China. They think it is not only inevitable because of globalization but also beneficial to both sides. As long as the quality and service are good, any brand from any country is accepted. This is a widespread attitude, and almost no officials have a different view on this issue.

Most of those who have had contact with American people hold positive views. Most officials feel that Americans are enthusiastic and open and that it is easier to understand and communicate with Americans than with people of other countries. Only about 20 percent believe that Americans are more self-centered than other nationalities.

In short, Chinese government officials' impressions of and views on the United States are complex. Most see the United States as neither good nor bad. Generally, they admire America's developed economy, advanced technology, strong legal and education systems, high standard of living, and inspiring domestic system. But they disagree with U.S. foreign policy, especially policy toward China, and are suspicious of U.S. hegemonic intentions. That said, most officials accept the United States as the most influential superpower and the leader of the Western world. If China is to develop its relations with Western countries and conform to international standards and norms, it must have a good relationship with the United States. China's fundamental interests in the twenty-first century are to realize modernization and to solve the problem of Taiwan, thus realizing unification of the motherland. These two problems cannot be achieved without the United States, and, therefore, China should work hard to address the differences and problems in the bilateral relationship.

Note

1. *Selected Works of Deng Xiaoping, 1982–1992,* vol. 3 (Beijing: Foreign Languages Press, 1994), p. 350.

CHAPTER FOUR

HOW TO VIEW U.S. STRATEGIC THINKING

Feng Changhong

STRATEGIC THINKING IS THE FOUNDATION of strategic decisionmaking. For a long time, U.S. strategic thinking has influenced its strategic decisionmaking. Chinese researchers who study the science of strategy (the "strategic circle") generally agree that U.S. strategic thinking has the characteristics of continuity and originality. In addition, because of constant changes in the domestic political situation and on the international stage, U.S. national interests are constantly evolving; therefore U.S. strategic thinking has the characteristic of adaptability, but also contradiction to some degree.

CONTENT OF U.S. STRATEGIC THINKING

U.S. strategic thinking is very active. It represents more than traditional strategic thinking of expansion and pragmatism; it is also based on concepts of national interest and global leadership. Chinese scholars understand that U.S. strategic thinking is unique and is based on a self-image as the primary decisionmaker in the world. The United States overemphasizes its own interests while it ignores the interests of others; it believes too much in its own strength and shows contempt toward the power of the international community; it pays too much attention to pragmatism but too little to its principles and commitments. In practice, the United States tends to act on its own and in a contradictory manner.

Supreme National Interests

The United States seldom considers the interests of the international community. Members of the Chinese strategic circle believe that this is because the United States holds its own national interests supreme above those of other nations and is committed to protecting or achieving those interests through military or nonmilitary means.

From the U.S. perspective, a top national interest is to safeguard national security. Although the United States, as the world's sole superpower, does not face serious challenges to its security, some people in the U.S. strategic circle believe that the United States is unsafe. They think that the post–Cold War era has brought about a series of serious challenges to the United States. Therefore, they must use political, economic, diplomatic, military, and ideological means to protect national security.

The United States defines its national security beyond its territorial borders, including in its security sphere any place where U.S. citizens live or U.S. national interests are at stake, regardless of issues of sovereignty or interests of the international community. In other words, U.S. strategic thinking is marked by unilateralism. If it is in its own interest, the United States will cooperate with the international community; if it is not, it might ignore international conventions or UN resolutions.

Another U.S. national interest is the promotion of economic prosperity and development. While strengthening its economic competitiveness, the United States tries to control the rules of the international economic order. People in the Chinese strategic circle argue that globalization has brought economic opportunities for all countries and that all nations should be able to participate fairly in the global economy. They believe the global economy should not be dominated by one power. The United States, however, persuades others to open their markets while it simultaneously practices trade protectionism.

The United States has significant influence in the three major international economic organizations: World Trade Organization (WTO), World Bank, and International Monetary Fund. At the same time, it practices unilateralism when it threatens trading partners with Super

301 sanctions. China will never deny America's right to develop its economy nor the fact that the United States has contributed greatly to world economic growth. However, the United States should promote global economic development in its real sense. In the process of globalization, the country with the greatest development has a duty to help developing countries achieve prosperity as well. Doing so will also help improve the international image of the United States.

The United States also views the spread of its values as a national interest. Just as the United States puts its interests above all others, it also holds it values higher as well. The United States believes that expanding democratic societies and free markets will further its strategic interests, a concept that was laid out in 1996 by President Bill Clinton in "A National Security Strategy of Engagement and Enlargement" and that is reflected even more vividly in the U.S.-led war on Iraq. Simply put, the United States wants to change Iraq into an Americanized democratic nation.

U.S. strategic thinking behind the Iraq war was based on the U.S. desire to promote its values and blend Iraq into Western society. Elsewhere, U.S. strategy is to accelerate the development of democracy and market reform in the former Soviet Union and Latin America, to help Central and Eastern European countries with economic reconstruction, to enlarge democratic camps in the Asia-Pacific region, and to help some African countries with democratization. The United States mobilizes all its international political, diplomatic, and economic influence to try to expand U.S.-style democracy. It seeks the spread of its value system and institutional changes.

Innate Mission of World Leadership

The United States possesses two competing traditions: realism and idealism. After the end of the Cold War, U.S. strategic thinking was dominated by idealism, when the United States embraced its "born mission" of shouldering a unique, God-entrusted responsibility for the development and destiny of human beings around the world. This concept would, therefore, make the United States superior to any other country and destined to lead the world. This sense of national superiority has been reinforced by both an American feeling of ethnic superiority and the typical American personality. Members of the Chinese strategic circle believe that the concepts of born mission and world leadership have greatly influenced U.S. governments and have become an important theoretical basis for strategic decisionmaking since the end of the Cold War.

On the basis of the concept of born mission, the United States seeks to establish a new world order under U.S. leadership. Chinese researchers in the science of strategy agree that all U.S. governments since the end of the Cold War have pursued a common mission: to be the world's leader, with all the benefits and responsibilities that come with it. In 1991, in his national security strategy report, President George H. W. Bush argued that a new world order should be established, with the United States in the lead, and that peace under U.S. governance should be achieved. President Clinton also stated that the United States must continue to exert influence as a world leader. The George W. Bush administration emphasized in its 2001 Quadrennial Defense Review that the United States should lead world politics, foreign affairs, and the global economy and that U.S. leadership will contribute to world peace, freedom, and prosperity. All three U.S. administrations stressed the responsibility of world leadership and shared the view that the stability of the post–Cold War world depends on U.S. leadership.

The United States seems determined to establish itself at the center of a new global political, economic, and military order. Chinese researchers of strategy believe, however, that the United States is engaging in wishful thinking and that its goals will not be acceptable to the international community. Obeying U.S. leadership would undermine the sovereignty and self-respect of countries around the world. If the United States tries to force its leadership through political, economic, or military means, it will spark conflict even with traditional allies. Therefore, it is clear that U.S. strategic thinking is not rational.

The United States also argues that human rights outweigh national sovereignty. The United States regularly interferes with other countries by criticizing their human rights records or supporting ethnic separatist forces. The United States has also sought to overthrow governments that are less democratic or that pay less respect to human rights. For example, NATO, led by the United States, used human rights as an excuse to launch a war against Yugoslavia, ultimately resulting in the breakup of a sovereign nation. Of course, the United States would never allow another country to do the same within its own borders. Americans seem to think that the United States should lead the world in solving the global human rights issue, but, in fact, human rights is an issue that should be addressed either by the sovereign leaders or under the umbrella of the UN.

The situation in Iraq provides another good example. The U.S. military has faced difficulties in Iraq in part because Americans misunderstand the relationship between human rights and sovereignty. In addition, U.S. strategic decisionmakers incorrectly estimated the determination of the Iraqi people. The Chinese government has resolutely stated that China will never interfere with other nations' sovereignty. China opposes using human rights to justify military intervention, and the United States should amend its strategic thinking accordingly.

Finally, the United States seeks to maintain leadership in the twenty-first century. This has been the core of U.S. strategic thinking since the end of the Cold War. When a problem cannot be resolved through non-military means, U.S. decisionmakers believe that the United States must use force or else risk undermining its image as the world leader. It is clear that the United States has decided to strengthen military construction, give prominence to military means, and build a strong deterrent against those it dislikes. The U.S. revolution in military affairs has enabled the United States to develop its military technology rapidly, which has helped the U.S. armed forces strike enemies with surgical precision and establish dominance in the military field.

The United States has not hesitated to break with traditional allies in its pursuit of global power. In other words, the United States is determined to lead the world even without international support. The war in Iraq was launched by the United States and Britain, over the disapproval—even objection—of Germany and France, two traditional allies. People in the Chinese strategic circle view this action as evidence that U.S. strategic thinking is capability based instead of threat based. In addition, the Iraq war reflects the fact that the Americans are overconfident and stubborn.

Military Pragmatism

America is known for its pragmatism, which has been evident since the earliest immigrants explored the wild new lands. The philosophical concept of pragmatism—the philosophy of the American spirit—has greatly influenced the country's politics, economy, and society as well as its strategic thinking. Pragmatism has grown into one of the fundamental concepts of U.S. strategic thinking since the end of the Cold War. The philosophical concept of pragmatism in the military field, with the epistemology of "usefulness is truth" and the methodology of "effect above principle" at its core, has exerted great influence on U.S. strategic decisionmaking.

First, the United States has adopted a flexible military strategy. According to U.S. strategic thinking, whatever is useful is correct. As long as military strategy can protect, consolidate, and expand U.S. national interests, it then can be adopted. Accordingly, U.S. military strategy may manifest itself in diverse ways, and later strategy can negate or contradict earlier ones.

U.S. strategy between the end of World War II and the end of the Cold War offers a good example of this principle. In every decade the United States instituted a new strategy—from containment to mass revenge to flexibility to realistic deterrence to new flexibility. Since the end of the Cold War, U.S. strategy has changed even more rapidly, with four specific military strategy adjustments over the course of a decade. The U.S. secretary of defense, Dick Cheney, adjusted U.S. military strategy to become the regional defense strategy in January 1993. In February 1995, General John Shalikashvili, chairman of the U.S. Joint Chiefs of Staff, announced the strategy of flexible and selective engagement in his annual report. In August 1997, Shalikashvili put forward "National Military Strategy: Shape, Respond, Prepare Now." In September 2002, the Bush administration formulated a U.S. national security strategy of preemptive strike—its military strategy in Iraq.

All these various military strategies are based on the philosophical concept of pragmatism. Their objectives are to serve U.S. national security interests. The strategy of preemptive strike, for example, openly states that the United States may launch the first blow against enemies before being attacked in order to safeguard its security, without consideration for international laws or rules.

In addition, the United States has adopted double standards. The United States applies pressure, imposes sanctions, or conducts military strikes only against those who are not in line with U.S. interests or are disliked by United States. For example, the United States took military action against the former Yugoslav government over the issue of Albanian self-rule in Kosovo but, at the same time, supports the Israeli position on the issue of Palestinian self-rule. The United States practiced double standards on other issues in Yugoslavia as well; it accused the Yugoslav government of ethnic cleansing but turned a blind eye toward the killing of Serbian civilians by Albanian militants. The United States accused Serb militants of "making a humanitarian disaster" but ignored human rights violations by the Kosovo Liberation Army.

The United States also has a double standard when it comes to the UN. When it needs the UN to exert influence, it works to manipulate the organization to support its objectives. When it finds the UN an obstacle, the United States simply bypasses it, launching unilateral military attacks with the help of a few allies. The United States started the first Gulf war in 1991, with UN authorization. It initiated the second war in the region without UN approval. The U.S. government seems to be able to justify these actions to itself, but people in the Chinese strategic circle regard these U.S. actions as overly pragmatic and based solely on what is most useful to U.S. interests at the time.

The United States also seeks to pursue the maximum war benefits. U.S. strategic thinking focuses on whether the benefits of going to war outweigh the costs—a very pragmatic outlook. However, this thinking leads policymakers to view military action as a means to achieve economic gains. Accordingly, wars that bring bonuses can be launched on a large scale; those that will not result in economic gains are passed over or waged on a small scale. The United States reaped significant economic benefits as a result of the 1991 Gulf War, for example. Germany, Japan, Kuwait, and Saudi Arabia together provided $13 billion in funding for the war, and other countries contributed many billions of dollars to the United States after the end of the war. Later, the United States sold the military equipment, new or used, that was provided for the Gulf War and also made a fortune in the follow-on reconstruction of Kuwait.

In the Kosovo War, the United States again reaped huge economic benefits. The U.S. government appropriated $15.1 billion, providing many commercial opportunities for American "merchants of death." Munitions were overstocked, and companies were provided a place to test their new, advanced weapons. In Kosovo, the United States "flew 60 percent of all combat sorties and dropped 80 percent of all precision-guided munitions."[1] Similarly, the United States has spent a fortune in the war against Iraq and will gain a huge economic reward in its reconstruction. These examples demonstrate that the United States views war in pragmatic terms, stressing war benefits over war costs.

STRATEGIC PERSPECTIVE AND EVALUATION IN SINO-U.S. RELATIONS

Chinese researchers of the science of strategy hold that the United States has long viewed China as an ideological rival, economic competitor, and potential military adversary. The United States uses ideology to distinguish friend from foe. Because the ideologies and social systems of China and the United States are vastly different, the United States views China, a leading socialist country, as a dissident rather than a normal partner in the international community. According to U.S. strategic thinking, China is a serious obstacle to U.S. efforts to promote democracy, freedom, and human rights around the world. From the Chinese perspective, U.S. strategic thinking severely hinders normal development of bilateral ties.

Chinese scholars of strategic science view the relationship as neither good nor bad, or as sometimes good and sometimes bad. These scholars believe that abandoning ideological differences and focusing on common interests is the best way to cultivate the relationship between the biggest developing country and the biggest developed country.

Realistic Economic Competitor

China's opening-up and reform have spurred its economic growth and put the Chinese economy onto a normal path of development. The U.S.

government has declared China an economic power that helps to maintain world peace and stability. Nonetheless, the United States is clearly wary of China's economic boom. U.S. strategic thinking posits that China's prosperity will ultimately endanger U.S. interests; therefore, China can be seen as an economic competitor. Put simply, the United States does not want China to surpass it economically. So far, China has no such capability, but some Americans are worried.

Americans who oppose China's rise want the U.S. government to limit economic exchange and cooperation with China, or even impose sanctions on China. This group knows little about China and overestimates the country's strength. As a result, members of this group view China as a rival rather than a friend. In fact, China's rise will have a positive impact on the United States. As friendly competitors, both the United States and China will help develop and strengthen each other's economies.

Potential Military Adversary

During the Cold War, the United States viewed the Soviet Union and Warsaw Pact countries as its major rivals. After the end of the Cold War and the disintegration of the Soviet bloc, the United States no longer had an obvious enemy. After the Gulf War, the United States shifted its strategic thinking about its major rival and replaced Russia—the major successor of the former Soviet Union—with China in that role. More recently, the Bush administration lowered bilateral relations from "constructive strategic partners"—the term used by the Clinton administration—to "constructive cooperative partners" to describe the U.S.-China relationship. This signals that changes in U.S. strategic thinking have taken place to the detriment to China.

China is not a major potential adversary of the United States and does not hope to engage in war with the United States. However, if the U.S. strategic circle does not stop viewing China as its main rival, sooner or later Chinese strategists will also begin to view the United States as their main rival—and a real rivalry will be created.

It is important that both sides engage in a strategic dialogue to communicate their perspectives on the other's strategic thinking. This will help build understanding and mutual trust between the two countries' strategic circles as well as friendship between the two peoples. As long as China and the United States understand and respect each other, there will be a better history between the two countries.

Note

1. Ivo H. Daalder, "The United States, Europe, and the Balkans" (Washington, D.C.: Brookings Institution, December 2000), p. 5, www.brook.edu/dybdocroot/views/articles/daalder/useurbalkch.pdf.

CHAPTER FIVE

FROM TWENTY TO FOUR

AMERICAN IMAGES IN A CHANGING CHINA

Lu Jiande

America is more like a world than a country: you could as well write a book about people, or about life.

—Martin Amis
The Moronic Inferno and Other Visits to America, 1987

THE UNITED STATES is indeed as many-sided and colorful as life itself, and therefore, the American image in China is difficult to describe. Instead of being a well-marked design, it is rather phantasmagoric, at once familiar and strange, always taking up interesting mutations. Hence, we can discuss "American images" rather than "the American image," as there is certainly more than one.

Since the Communist takeover of China in 1949, "Uncle Sam" has been a poorly formulated in China. Crude official anti-imperialist and anti-American propaganda backfired in that it stirred up a strong undercurrent of pro-American sentiment among Chinese artists and intellectuals. Pro-Americanism came out into the open after the normalization of diplomatic relations between the two countries in 1979, and it grew in the late 1980s and early 1990s as a result of both domestic turmoil in China and an enthusiastic if somewhat naive belief in the universality of American values. However, familiarity produces neglect, if not disillusionment. Recently, Chinese impressions of the United States have been perilously set in a different direction. This development is hardly the direct result of incidents like the embassy bombing in Yugoslavia in 1999 and the EP-3 air collision over Hainan Island in 2001. Rather, it is entangled with China's critical review of its own vehemently idealistic past and the strain of radicalism in American national life. In other words, U.S. images in China are ultimately connected to the way China perceives itself.

U.S. RADICALISM AND GROWING CHINESE REALISM

There is no need to retell modern Chinese history, but U.S. radicalism calls for some explanation. Henry Steele Commager, author of *The American Mind* (1951) and a prolific American historian who in 1941 inaugurated the teaching of U.S. history at the University of Cambridge, England, offers a telling example of American radicalism. When describing the national character of Britain through American eyes, Commager compared typical English and American attitudes, noting that, of some 25 Cambridge colleges, only three were for women. "When it was observed, recently, that the number was scarcely sufficient, there was prompt agreement: there should be, said a young don, at least four. An American would have said, almost automatically, that there should be twenty."[1]

Here, on the one hand, we have the English handicapped by their legendary conservatism; on the other, we have Americans blessed with a firm grasp of the modern view of equality between men and women. Reading this anecdote, we are at first shocked by the English don who seems to be lacking in both youthful vigor and a decent respect for women's equal rights to higher education. On second thought, however, we might find the American expression of immediate numerical justice just short of revolutionary. Would Cambridge, town and gown, be prepared for such an unexpected expansion? How to raise the funds to cover the cost of land and the expenditure on buildings? When artificially set up, would these colleges still have their own characteristics, a result of organic historical growth? Should academic standards be lowered if there is a shortage of qualified candidates? Where would competent governing bodies and mistresses for these new colleges be found? In short, the don is quick to see the absurdity of a patriarchal society as reflected in its educational system and acknowledges the necessity of reform. But he suspects that Cambridge, or even England, has not the necessary material and means at its command for this egalitarian task. So his conservative recommendation of at least one more women's college has the saving grace of being workable.

Many contemporary Chinese readers, so used to jerky movements of various kinds, would probably side with the American in this attempt to redress a historical wrong. If the university is a microcosm of society, the American can be seen as a daring Jacobin.

The Chinese know this radical attitude only too well. For quite a long time, radicalism was the trademark of Chinese political correctness: all links to traditional Chinese culture were to be severed; the most beautiful picture is drawn on a clean sheet. Mao would have no patience for English gradualism. In one of his poems, Mao asked his followers to stay away from a slow approach: "Oh no, ten thousand years? It's too long. / Make it, here and now." Mao's Great Leap Forward was a result of this radical and unrealistic thinking.

While it is possible that Commager exaggerated the divide within the Anglo-Saxon world, many Chinese find his characterization pertinent. More often than not, Americans tend to be radicals when they are talking about reform programs in other countries—especially countries that are not favorably viewed by standards of American democratic ideals or geopolitical interests; and this radicalism often underlies U.S. foreign policy and (lack of) diplomacy.

The polarity of the two positions corresponds to two kinds of people in the history of political ideas. One group of people can be described as robust optimists. They believe that human beings are naturally good and perfectible; should there be any problems, it is society that is to blame because all evils arise from irrational and bad social and political arrangements. By the sheer force of willpower and pure reason, we can build a "people's commune" or a "new Jerusalem," which promises an immediate relief of all sufferings. This group of people also has monist visions of reality. They believe that values are coherent and compatible and that there is a set of universal, overarching standards by which all cultures and institutions can be evaluated. Consequently, in this view, there is also a final solution to conflicts of values.

The other group sees human beings as flawed and fallible. Members of this group would agree with Immanuel Kant: "Out of timber so crooked as that from which man is made, nothing entirely straight can be built."[2] People in this category are not very confident that history is ever in progress or that an iron law governs historical development. If the existing system is not working very well or in keeping with time, it can only be changed in a gentle manner, gradually and cautiously, just in case grave side effects would arise. These people do not look down upon piecemeal readjustments and local corrections that are, in contrast, denounced by a Chinese revolutionary doctrinaire as "minced steps of an old lady with bound feet." Reforms of the practical kind are long and well-sustained processes; the effect of each step is closely watched. A Chinese saying sums up this empiricist position: "Wade across the river by feeling out for stones"—take one step and look around before taking another. This group of people is also pluralistic. They hold that equally desirable values are not necessarily compatible; one must not judge one culture by the criteria of another; differing civilizations embody different ways of living and pursue different goals.

If formerly the Chinese, in their ambitious utopian dreams, would respond warmly to the American "twenty," now they have started to appreciate the maturity and realism of the British "four." They are no longer easily incited by "paradise now" and would have serious doubts about all the grand narratives, whether of the nineteenth century or today. This does not mean that they are satisfied by the status quo in China. Instead, they have a sense of urgency in the face of numerous social problems. Taught by the bitter and bloody experiences of the Soviet Union, they understand that long-growing problems of a country like China are a tangled business. The Chinese are also examining orthodox universalistic ideals and the monistic presumption of human and social progress. Under the influence of the idea of cultural diversity and American theories of multiculturalism, they have come to see that different societies and their ideals are often incommensurable: "Such questions as which of them is the best, or even which one should prefer, which one should judge to be nearer to the universal human ideal . . . are, therefore . . . in the end meaningless."[3]

THE BEHOLDER

A study of beauty is lame without a study of the beholder. American images in China have gone through subtle transformations as China has reevaluated its own modern radical past.

In the nineteenth century, of all foreign countries, the United States was viewed by Chinese most positively. The history of the United States offered inspiration to many Chinese radicals and men of letters. In 1848, when the American poet, Ralph Waldo Emerson, was delivering his lectures on the English traits and Emperor Dao Guang's reign came to its 28th year, Xu Jiyu finished his *Ying Huan Zhi Lue*, one of the earliest Chinese books on world history and geography.[4] In this book, George Washington is described as combining the power of a demigod and the virtues of a Confucian gentleman. An American missionary working in Ningbo had Xu's elegant description of the first U.S. president inscribed on a piece of granite and shipped back to his country. The construction of an obelisk dedicated to Washington had just begun, and Xu's eulogy to the American hero was inserted in the interior walls in that monument.

Because of events following the Boxer Rebellion (1900), China was plunged into misery and humiliation at the turn of the century. It was at this moment of crisis that new concepts were invoked for China's meteoric rise. Terms like republic, democracy, revolution, and liberty made their way to China via Japan and were all of a sudden endowed with magic power. The story of American freedom unfolded in its Chinese version, and Washington's name, like Rousseau's, became a symbol of liberty and revolution.

In 1903, Zou Rong, an eighteen-year-old from Sichuan, published *Ge Ming Jun* [Revolution army], which at the time was an extremely influential pamphlet of revolutionary propaganda and contributed to the end of the feudal system in China. Its current obscurity reveals a major change in style, ideology, and Chinese projection of American images.

It is hard to imagine that *Ge Ming Jun* could still captivate the young Chinese reading public. Scrutiny of the text demonstrates that it is actually a hodgepodge of disconnected and plagiarized ideas, full of sound and fury, signifying nothing. This piece of hatred, bitterness, and adolescent aspirations is cluttered with poetic touches. If there is a shortage of well-prepared arguments, it abounds in abstract phraseology and sonorous clichés. Small wonder, then, that the author not only is enshrined in China's history of revolution but also occupies a place in the pantheon of modern Chinese literature.

What, then, is Zou's immediate source of inspiration? He had just read the Chinese translation of the U.S. Declaration of Independence and considered it the bible for all countries. U.S. historians over the past two decades have convincingly shown that, contrary to popular belief, this 1776 declaration served a very practical purpose—to give legitimacy to French intervention in the British colonies. Therefore, in the eighteenth century, the Declaration of Independence did not have the kind of monumental resonance it now enjoys. It was only in the nineteenth century, when Americans were in need of an untroubled faith in their country's extraordinary birth (an immaculate conception, without the taint of original sin, so to speak), that the declaration acquired a great significance.

Toward the end of *Ge Ming Jun,* sections of Declaration of Independence were appropriated and images of the American revolution, the flag of independence, the Liberty Bell, the hall of independence, Bunker Hill, and the Statue of Liberty were strewn over the text. In Zou's vision of the future Chinese republic, the organization of the government, the constitution, and the legal system should all copy the United States.[5] Zou believed that inalienable rights are not historically and culturally contingent; they are universals. When the U.S. style of liberty would prevail in China, all the sufferings and hardships would disappear. What was wanted was a replacement for the complex, traditional Chinese customs governing the social order of 1903 by simple, elementary rules borrowed from foreign countries.

In China, the first three decades of the twentieth century were an age of nihilistic extremism. Young radicals were arrogantly sure that the most thorough revolution would start from consciousness. Hence the Chinese language was to be taken over by Esperanto, all the cumbrous forms and hoary archaisms were to be trimmed away. A disinherited mind, a tabula rasa, so to speak, would be the mind for the future.

Zou and many after him would attribute U.S. success solely to the ideals embodied in the U.S. Declaration of Independence and Constitution. When better equipped with historical knowledge, Chinese intellectuals realized that without the strong support of institutions these documents are merely words on paper. On the other hand, Alexis de Tocqueville, author of *Democracy in America,* is responsible for misleadingly attributing many different effects in the United States to the principle of equality. Even earlier, Adam Smith shrewdly observed in his classic work, *An Inquiry into the Nature and Causes of the Wealth of Nations* (1776) on the eve of the American Revolution: "The colony of a civilized nation, which takes possession either of a waste country, or of one so thinly inhabited, that the natives easily give place to the new settlers, advances more rapidly to wealth and greatness than any other human society."[6] The sagacity of the American founders is undeniable, but it is also clear that American success is the result of a lucky combination of historical factors. Richard Rorty, one of the most articulate American pragmatists of the present day, argues that American values and institutions are contingent upon a given set of circumstances, which are not repeatable.

The revolution that overthrew the Qing dynasty in 1911 was strikingly similar to the French Revolution in the sense that men of letters played a very important role. When the old regime was toppled, revolutionaries had nothing concrete to say. Writing in *The Ancient Regime and the French Revolution* (1856), de Tocqueville offered a critique of literary radicals:

> Our men of letters did not merely impart their revolutionary ideas to the French nation; they also shaped the national temperament and outlook on life. In the long process of molding men's minds to their ideal pattern their task was all the easier since the French had had no training in the field of politics, and they thus had a clear field. The result was that our writers ended up by giving the Frenchman the instincts, the turn of mind, the tastes, and even the eccentricities characteristic of the literary man. And when the time came for action, these literary propensities were imported into the political arena.
>
> When we closely study the French Revolution we find that it was conducted in precisely the same spirit as that which gave rise to so many books

expounding theories of government in the abstract. Our revolutionaries had the same fondness for broad generalizations, cut-and-dried legislative systems, and a pedantic symmetry; the same contempt for hard facts; the same taste for reshaping institutions on novel, ingenious, original lines; the same desire to reconstruct the entire constitution according to the rules of logic and a preconceived system instead of trying to rectify its faulty parts. The result was nothing short of disastrous; for what is a merit in the writer may well be a vice in the statesman and the very qualities which go to make great literature can lead to catastrophic revolutions.[7]

While French men of letters of the Enlightenment contributed so brilliantly to literature, philosophy, and the history of ideas, Zou Rong left to posterity only a collection of angry phrases. Totally unacquainted with the world he was determined to destroy and inexperienced in all its affairs, he ultimately had nothing to say. What Zou was advocating is actually a systematic, simultaneous abolition of all existing laws and customs. Its admirers were to be its victims; they had not the least presentiments of this. They nursed the foolish hope that a sudden, radical transformation of an ancient, highly intricate social system could be brought about with one fatal thrust of the dagger to the Qing dynasty, and the star of liberty would shine over the land of Cathay.

DEFINING LIBERTY

U.S. images in China are also mediated by translations of Western works, classical and popular, that have been conspicuously displayed in Chinese bookstores. Exposure to works criticizing the French Revolution, for example, has changed Chinese views of their revolutionary past. Similarly, images of the United States are somewhat affected by this process of self-scrutiny and soul searching. The development of a discourse of liberty and revolution is strangely separated from stubborn social realities. The terms themselves are reduced to buzzwords. You proclaim liberty, and people are instantly free; you declare liberation, and people are once and for all liberated. It is this kind of atmospheric rhetoric against which Chinese intellectuals have come to be vigilant.

The orator Patrick Henry is believed to have said in one of the most celebrated speeches during the American Revolution: "Give me liberty or give me death."[8] Liberty seems to be a finished business, as absolute as death. This untroubled belief in abstract liberty is shorn of historical and social content. For Zou Rong and his comrades, concrete issues are forever secondary. The term liberty has an essence, in isolation of social relationships, ready made and self-contained.

The relevance of the English attitude to social change must not be overlooked. In Britain, there is no lack of eccentrics dedicated to social engineering. But even a radical thinker like Jeremy Bentham would find the French inclination toward generalities and universals offensive. He was made an honorary citizen of the newly founded French Republic, but he ruthlessly demolished the Declaration of Rights, which he considered too abstract, exaggerated, and imprecise.

In temperament and politics, Bentham was markedly dissimilar from his countryman, Edmund Burke. But the Utilitarian designer of "Panopticon," a scheme for the better management of prisons, and the staunch critic of the French Revolution share something in common: a typically British dislike for the abstract. The French preference for liberty over peace and order shocked Burke. In his letter to M. Dupont, Burke wrote:

> Of all the loose terms in the world, liberty is the most indefinite. It is not solitary, unconnected, individual, selfish liberty, as if every man was to regulate the whole of his conduct by his own will. The liberty I mean is social freedom. It is the state of things in which liberty is secured by the equality of restraint. A constitution of things in which the liberty of no one man, and no body of men, and no number of men, can find means to trespass on the liberty of any person, or any description of persons, in the society. This kind of liberty is, indeed, but another name for justice; ascertained by wise laws, and secured by well-constructed institutions.[9]

To be enjoyed, then, liberty should be combined with "government; with public force; with the discipline and obedience of armies; with the collection of an effective and well-distributed revenue; with morality and religion; with the solidity of property; with peace and order; with civil and social manners."[10] Without all these good things, liberty is not a benefit and is not likely to continue long. In Burke's view, we would hesitate to say a country liberated from a dictator is free because we have to examine whether civil life has returned to normal. It is to be noted that communism has been denounced by many for its sacrifice of the present for an uncertain future.

To Burke, the state of liberty has no clear-cut demarcation lines. Even under the rule of the ancient regime, Burke argued, the French people enjoyed a considerable degree of civil liberties. Unlike the French thinkers of the Enlightenment, Burke and his concept of liberty are surprisingly ahead of their time. Put in our present language: liberty is culturally embedded and more or less relativistic. Because the liberties and the restrictions vary with times and circumstances and admit of infinite modifications, they cannot be settled upon any abstract rule; and nothing is so foolish as to discuss them upon that principle.[11]

Burke would say that, in many places in the world, people are not ripe for liberty. "Men are qualified for civil liberty in exact proportion to their disposition to put moral chains upon their own appetites; in proportion as their love to justice is above their rapacity; in proportion as their soundness and sobriety of understanding is above their vanity and presumption." Michael Sandel, a Harvard philosopher, states that liberty will last only when there is self-government informed with a sharing of civic virtues. Therefore, reform of any value would be long and slow.

Modern Chinese intellectuals have generally not been familiar with this line of thinking. Moderation is stigmatized as the trademark of cowards. The gradualist approach encapsulated in "There should at least be four" is beyond our imagination. Radicalism, once so heartily applauded by Americans, has fortunately come to a peaceful demise in the United States. But there is a very important caveat. Americans are extremely accomplished in the art of compromise in their own country. They would not mold their country in total accordance with an abstruse theory fabricated in a remote country.

Chinese intellectuals are indebted to the United States along nonidealistic lines as well. In an age of extremes, Hu Shih stood for humaneness and sobriety. He was a conscientious promoter of American pragmatism and served as China's ambassador to the United States during World War II. As a liberal, he initially advocated wholesale Westernization and a radical cultural revolution. Like his mentor, John Dewey, Hu discouraged young students from seeking universal formulas or pana-ceas for all China's problems. His advice was that individual problems should be individually solved; and solid studies of problems are more valuable than empty talks of "-isms." What we are in need of, he urged, is down-to-earth fieldwork rather than hasty imports of social or polit-ical theories.

Unfortunately, the popularity of foreign "-isms" and "-cracies" in China is both a death sentence for social amelioration and an eyewit-ness to intellectual bankruptcy. The attraction to abstract theories proved fatal, but it was revitalized 20 years ago because of American encouragement. Gradually, Chinese intellectuals have discovered that the American media like short and pithy slogans because the American audience has no time for detailed analysis of complicated social prob-lems in a foreign country. Declare yourself a champion for democracy and human rights, and you win the hearts of tens of thousands of polit-ically gullible Americans. It is this American mental laziness that has been ruthlessly exploited by people who love neither the United States nor China. China's current challenges are legion—pervasive disregard for rules, collapse of professional ethics, increasing disparity between rich and poor, unprecedented environmental pollution, and deplor-able implementation of justice, to name just a few. To pontificate about democratic ideals in certain situations is like tickling famine refugees.

ACCEPTING CULTURAL DIVERSITY

In this age of so-called globalization, Chinese intellectuals are strongly in favor of an international exchange of ideas among the nations, but they are also deeply concerned with the issue of cultural diversity. They complain that the dominance of the English language is the principal agent in the destruction of linguistic diversity.

To accept diversity requires great effort, generosity of spirit, and imagination. It is understandable that many people, from both sides of the Pacific, might forget how different the United States and China are and expect the other country to behave as it would. In China, many view U.S. propaganda as highly sophisticated and effective. Thanks to easy access to the Internet and Western media and to authors from

Huntington to Chomsky, Chinese intellectuals are now sensitive to discourses of representations and interpretations, to hidden interests coached in deceptive language, and to the politically convenient uses of blanket terms (like "pro-democracy") at the expense of facts not easily digestible.

If the language of liberty worked well on Chinese university campuses some 15 years ago, it now looks tired and embarrassed. The image of the United States as the beacon of freedom is seriously tarnished. The United States is seen as a spendthrift, squandering its political capital. Many Chinese even suspect that the United States does not care much about its own image abroad, preferring to go its own way.

Checks and balances are desirable internationally as well as domestically. In a much anthologized speech (available in Chinese), a U.S. federal judge, Learned Hand, interpreted the spirit of freedom as a capacity for self-doubt, a willingness to understand other points of view, and a habitually disinterested consideration of one's own interests and others' interests. If this spirit of freedom prevails, the United States will be loved rather than held in awe, and its images in China would be most endearing.

Notes

1. Henry Steele Commager, ed., *Britain Through American Eyes* (London: Bodley Head, 1974), p. 757.

2. This dictum has been widely popularized in Isaiah Berlin, *The Crooked Timber of Humanity: Chapters in the History of Ideas,* ed. Henry Hardy (New York: Knopf, 1991), much of which is devoted to scathing criticisms of the Marxist doctrine of historical inevitability.

3. Isaiah Berlin, *Vico and Herder: Two Studies in the History of Ideas* (London: Hogarth, 1976), p. 210. This is Berlin again rehearsing J. G. von Herder, a harbinger of the Romantic movement. Herder's theory of culture, in his time, was a powerful corrective of the often too thin and artificial universalism of the Enlightenment. To the surprise of many Chinese intellectuals, U.S. democracy and old-style communism are both the product of the Enlightenment.

4. Also in 1848, the United States had just won the Mexican War and, as a result, annexed more than one million square kilometers of land. At the same time, the phrase "manifest destiny" was taking root in popular U.S. political imagination.

5. Zou's friend and teacher, Zhang Taiyan, would name this new oriental republic the United Provinces of China. Zou did not live to see the downfall of the rule of the Manchus.

6. Adam Smith, *Wealth of Nations* (1776), in *Glasgow Edition of the Works and Correspondence of Adam Smith*, vol. 3, ed. A. S. Skinner and E. H. Campbell (Indianapolis: Liberty Fund, 1981), chap. 7, part 2, http://oll.libertyfund.org/Texts/LF-Books/Smith0232/GlasgowEdition/WealthOfNations/0141-03_Bk.html#toc_lf0141.3.head.005.

7. Alexis de Tocqueville, *The Ancient Regime and the French Revolution*, trans. Stuart Gilbert (Garden City, N.Y.: Doubleday, 1955), p. 168.

8. The quote was actually penned by his biographer years after his death.

9. Harold Laski, ed., *Letters of Edmund Burke: A Selection* (London: Oxford University Press, 1922), p. 269.

10. Edmund Burke, *Reflections on the Revolution in France*, ed. Conor Cruise O'Brien (New York: Viking Penguin, 1969), pp. 90–91.

11. Ibid., p. 151.

PART THREE

POPULAR VIEWS OF THE UNITED STATES

CHAPTER SIX

CHINESE VIEWS OF AMERICA
A SURVEY

Zhao Mei

SINCE 2000, the Institute of American Studies (IAS) at the Chinese Academy of Social Sciences (CASS) has engaged in the project, "Chinese See America," in China. In March–April 2000 and in June–July 2001, the project conducted surveys through the use of questionnaires, symposia, telephone calls, and face-to-face interviews.[1] Our goal was to gauge the views of various segments of the Chinese public about America and learn how the views were formed so that we could work to minimize misunderstanding and misconception.

In 2004, working with the Center for Strategic and International Studies (CSIS), IAS participated in the research project, "Chinese Images of the United States." From February to April 2004, on the basis of our previous surveys, we conducted a survey with questionnaires and interviews in Beijing, Shanghai, Xiamen, Guangzhou, Shenzhen, Nanning, Zhuhai, and Chengdu. We sent out 1,000 questionnaires and received 886 replies. On April 6, 2004, 13 Chinese journalists participated in our symposium in Beijing on America's image in Chinese media. The open, free discussions expanded our thought and deepened our understanding of the survey results.

As a preliminary summary of the survey results, this report represents views of America from some sectors in the Chinese population. Owing to practical limitations, the following factors may have affected in various ways the accuracy of the survey results:

- Our survey focused on government officials, journalists, college students, academics, and businesspeople. Most have a college or postgraduate education and live in cities. Some have lived or worked in the United States. Their views of America may be different from those of peasants, migrant workers, other professionals, and unemployed urban residents. Our sample groups represent the scope of our contacts with the general population.

- Because we depended heavily on volunteers in Shanghai, Beijing, and Guangzhou and because the questionnaires were sent and received through the postal office and via e-mail, the survey took a month, instead of a few days, to complete. International and domestic events taking place during this period could have affected respondents' views of the United States.

- We are not professional pollsters although we had conducted two similar surveys before. Our lack of experience could have affected the framing of questions, quantification of results, and conclusions.

In spite of these limitations, we have striven to present a quantitative analysis of the representative views of the United States held by Chinese people. As in previous surveys, the latest survey indicates that respondents, regardless of their location, profession, and age, give consistent answers to some questions yet disagree on other questions. Therefore, their answers and the thinking behind them to a large extent reflect public opinion.

Our report has four parts. Part one looks at general Chinese views of the United States, including impressions of America and Americans, opinions on U.S. influence in the world, and issues like willingness to study in the United States. Part two deals with opinions on American domestic and foreign policy, including the U.S. war on terrorism, U.S. political and economic systems, and U.S. culture. Part three focuses on issues related to Sino-American relations such as the Taiwan issue, U.S.-China trade, and the future of Sino-American relations. The final section analyzes the survey results and compares the conclusions with two early surveys and other Chinese polls and publications on the United States.

PART ONE: GENERAL VIEWS OF AMERICA

Important developments in the United States, in Sino-American relations, and in China clearly influenced our respondents. Their views of America are shaped by both the legacy of the past and recent events. The following is an overview of relevant events during the period between our prior survey in June–July 2001 and the April 2004 survey.

- U.S. domestic developments include the September 11 terrorist attacks; economic recession since 2001; stricter immigration and visa policies since 9/11; the Enron bankruptcy in December 2001; the establishment of the Department of Homeland Security in January 2003; and the 2004 presidential campaign.

- International developments and those related to Sino-American relations include the U.S.-led war in Afghanistan launched in October 2001; President Bush's 2002 State of the Union address in which he called North Korea, Iran, and Iraq an "axis of evil"; Bush's declaration of his preemption strategy in 2002; U.S. withdrawal from the antiballistic missile treaty and U.S. development of a missile defense system; the U.S.-led war on Iraq in March 2003; the failure of the WTO Cancun meeting and the rising antiglobalization movement; the Beijing meeting in April 2003 of the United States, North Korea, and China on the nuclear issue and the following rounds of six-party talks; the rise of the U.S. trade deficits with China; Premier Wen Jiabao's visit to Washington in December 2003; and the U.S. human rights resolution against China in the UN meeting in Geneva in April 2004.

- Chinese domestic developments include the Communist Party's 16th Congress that selected the new leadership; the outbreak of SARS in some regions of China in the spring of 2003; the continuous growth of China's economy; and the amendments to China's constitution in March 2004.

These events undoubtedly affected our respondents' views of the United States, albeit to different degrees. Note that many respondents offered more than one answer to some questions in the questionnaire. Some chose not to answer certain questions for they thought they were

Table 1. Question: What is your opinion of America?

Respondents	Generally favorable: developed economy, rule of law, democracy, fair foreign policy	Generally unfavorable: economic polarization, racism, phony democracy, overbearing foreign policy	Mixed: high standard of living, good domestic system, hegemony in internat'l affairs, imprudent China policy	Not sure: it's too compli-cated
Journalists	24.13	3.44	63.79	10.34
College students	16.08	4.77	69.60	9.55
Government officials	15.53	8.74	70.87	4.37
Business-people	17.22	5.30	68.87	8.61
People from academia	38.89	5.56	55.56	0.00
Others	7.69	11.54	73.08	7.69
Average	13.66	5.68	68.62	8.19

not appropriately worded. Some made changes to the questions. For example, they crossed out "strongly" from "strongly oppose" in the question about the U.S. war in Iraq. All data on tables are percentages.

In short, the survey found that, consistent with findings from the previous surveys, the most prominent characteristic of Chinese views of America is love-hate ambivalence. Overwhelming majorities had mixed views of the United States as a country of "inward democracy and outward overbearingness," as one respondent noted. This is a consensus view among all groups. As a group, however, academics showed a higher percentage holding mostly favorable views of America (see table 1).

Views of Americans

Majorities of journalists, college students, and academics generally thought of Americans as warm, open, and accessible. The average also shows this result (table 2).

Table 2. Question: In your contact with foreigners, what is your impression of Americans?

Respondents	Warm and open, more accessible and easier to understand than people from other countries	Self-centered rarely consider others' interests and feelings	Not too much different from other Westerners	Aloof and and stiff, not very accessible
Journalists	60.34	10.34	29.31	0.00
College students	55.73	16.67	25.78	1.82
Government officials	42.86	21.16	35.98	0.00
Business-people	47.30	14.19	35.81	2.70
People from academia	66.67	16.67	16.67	0.00
Others	38.46	26.92	30.77	3.85
Average	52.22	16.43	30.02	1.31

Studying in the United States

When asked, "What will you do if you or your children have a chance to study in America?" more than two-thirds of respondents answered, "I'd like to go, but it also depends on circumstances." More people from the academic group chose the answer, "I will go without hesitation" than from other groups (table 3).

PART TWO: VIEWS OF AMERICAN DOMESTIC AND FOREIGN POLICIES

Previous survey results have shown that Chinese views of America are complex and ambivalent. Those who view the United States favorably see a country of high technology, economic prosperity, and cultural diversity with the ability to attract talent from all over the world. Those who view the United States unfavorably consider U.S. behavior

Table 3. Question: What will you do if you (or your children) have a chance to study in America?

Respondents	I will go without hesitation	I'd like to go, but it depends on circumstances (financial aid, selection of school and subject of study, etc.)	I'm not interested and would rather stay in China	Never thought about it
Journalists	15.55	68.97	1.72	13.79
College students	12.81	77.14	4.77	5.28
Government officials	14.56	58.25	12.14	15.05
Business-people	18.67	54.00	12.67	14.67
People from academia	38.89	55.56	0.00	5.56
Others	7.69	73.08	7.69	11.54
Average	14.92	67.57	7.08	10.44

in international affairs as arrogant and overbearing. This survey focuses on Chinese views of the war in Iraq, the U.S. political system and economic order, and U.S. cultural products.

America's Role in the World

Since *The Rise and Fall of the Great Powers: Economic Change and Military Conflict from 1500 to 2000*[2] was translated into Chinese in 1990, there has been a persistent interest in China in America's status as a global power. The reflection on and discussion of this question among Chinese government officials, scholars, even ordinary people have become heightened because of developments like the September 11 attacks, the strategy of preemption and neoimperialism, worldwide anti-Americanism, and the publication in China of *The Tragedy of Great Power Politics*.[3]

Table 4. Question: What do you think will happen with the United States?

Respondents	Will continue to be prosperous and be the only superpower for a long time	Has started declining and will soon become one of the poles in a multipolar world	Its powerful position is temporary; it has become more isolated and its global influence is declining	Hard to tell whether relative power of U.S. will grow or decline
Journalists	37.93	1.72	46.55	15.51
College students	33.59	8.84	40.70	12.88
Government officials	37.50	7.69	40.87	13.94
Business-people	29.14	4.64	52.98	13.25
People from academia	33.33	11.11	38.89	16.67
Others	4.00	4.00	64.00	28.00
Average	33.68	6.65	48.88	14.06

Survey results show divided opinion. Some believed that U.S. power is temporary, that it has become more isolated, and that its global influence is in decline. Others believed that the United States will continue to be prosperous and the only superpower for a long time to come. Only a minority of respondents thought that America has started declining or that it is hard to tell whether U.S. power will grow or decline (table 4).

The War in Iraq

Opinions were very divided on the issue of the Iraq war. Support for war was highest among academics, while opposition was strongest among journalists. More than 50 percent, on average, believed that it was reasonable to overthrow Saddam but that resorting to war was wrong. Those who supported the war or felt indifferent to it were in the minority (table 5).

Table 5. Question: What is your attitude to America's war in Iraq?

Respondents	Support	Oppose	It was reasonable to overthrow Saddam, but the resort to war was wrong	It just happened and was irrelevant to us
Journalists	10.34	55.17	53.44	0.00
College students	6.55	33.75	54.41	5.29
Government officials	9.62	39.90	45.19	5.29
Business-people	3.31	41.06	49.01	6.62
People from academia	22.22	16.67	55.56	5.56
Others	0.00	44.00	52.00	4.00
Average	7.45	39.75	51.35	4.59

American Domestic Politics

Most respondents care somewhat and have some understanding of America's domestic issues, such as its two political parties, the presidential election, race relations, immigration policy, and tax and financial issues. The groups showed little difference in their answers to this question (table 6).

American Democracy and Market Economy

Two-thirds of respondents believed that American democracy and its market economy "suit American conditions and bring prosperity and stability, but they do not necessarily suit developing countries." This answer was consistent with previous survey results; only the 2000 and 2001 surveys gave a more favorable rating to America's economic system. The majority answer in 2004—that the U.S. system may not suit developing countries—reflected the thinking provoked by corporate scandals in America in recent years.

It is noteworthy that journalists showed the highest percentage of those who believe that American democracy and the market economy

Table 6. Question: What is your opinion of American domestic issues (party politics, presidential elections, racial relations, immigration policy, tax and financial policies, social welfare)?

Respondents	Don't care and am not interested	Have some knowledge and interest	Hard to understand because U.S. and Chinese politics are so different	Not much different from other countries' politics; little more than power game for the rich
Journalists	0	81.03	3.45	15.51
College students	10.58	65.49	6.30	17.63
Government officials	9.85	57.64	13.79	18.72
Business-people	11.92	45.03	18.54	24.50
People from academia	5.56	50.00	16.67	27.78
Others	4.00	28.00	20.00	48.00
Average	8.60	61.89	9.92	19.59

suit only America, while the academic group had the highest percentage who believe that American democracy and the market economy have universal significance and deserve study (table 7).

American Culture

Majorities had favorable views of American culture (literature, arts, music, movies, and television). However, some prefer Chinese culture because of the irrelevance of American culture to their lives. Others, on the other hand, like American culture and think it produces excellent work. Only a minority of respondents thought of American culture as biased or trite (table 8).

Table 7. Question: What do you think about America's democratic system and market economy?

Respondents	Phony democracy only for the rich; not fair competition	Suit U.S. conditions and bring prosperity and stability; but do not necessarily suit developing countries	Have universal significance and deserve study and borrowing	Compare unfavorably with some other Western countries with better welfare systems
Journalists	3.44	77.58	6.89	15.51
College students	12.09	65.49	18.64	3.78
Government officials	7.88	64.53	20.69	6.90
Business-people	6.62	62.25	23.84	7.28
People from academia	5.56	50.00	38.89	5.56
Others	11.54	57.69	19.23	11.54
Average	8.75	66.29	18.34	7.19

PART THREE: VIEWS OF SINO-AMERICAN RELATIONS

Our survey focused on opinions on U.S.-China trade frictions, Taiwan, and the future of Sino-American relations. Answers indicate problems in Sino-American relations and the confusion that many Chinese feel regarding America's actions since 9/11.

Outlook for Sino-American Relations

Opinions on this question were divided. The belief in gradual improvement in Sino-American relations claimed the highest average percentage, followed by keeping the status quo, conflicts in the future, and uncertainty about the answer (table 9).

Table 8. Question: What do you think about American cultural products (literature, arts, pop music, movies, and television)?

Respondents	OK, but distant from my life; I prefer Chinese cultural products	Biased and always promote U.S. values; I don't like them	Enjoy them very much; many are exquisite	Most are trite and too commercialized; inferior to European and Chinese classics
Journalists	37.93	3.44	43.10	12.06
College students	32.41	10.80	39.70	17.09
Government officials	47.03	9.90	34.65	8.42
Business-people	47.65	4.03	37.58	10.74
People from academia	38.89	5.56	44.44	11.11
Others	65.38	3.85	11.54	19.23
Average	39.84	8.03	38.18	13.36

Taiwan

Taiwan has always been one of the most sensitive issues in Sino-American relations. The survey question focused on the motives behind the Taiwan policy of the United States. Results showed wide differences among groups. Three U.S. motives—create obstacles to China's rise, turn Taiwan into America's unsinkable aircraft, and fulfill America's international obligation—each received agreement, on average, from between one-quarter and one-third of the respondents. Approximately 15 percent of those surveyed believe that the U.S. motive is support of Taiwan's democracy. The results also show journalists ranked "fulfill international obligation" first, while the academic group put "create obstacles in China's rising" on top (table 10).

Table 9. Question: How do you see the prospects for the relationship between China and the United States?

Respondents	Conflicts exist, but gradual improvement will take place	Status quo will remain, with ups and downs	U.S. will not allow China to become a great power, so there will be serious conflicts in the future	Hard to say; there are too many variables
Journalists	46.55	32.75	17.24	3.45
College students	38.19	23.87	22.61	15.33
Government officials	34.95	24.27	31.55	9.22
Business-people	34.44	32.45	19.87	13.25
People from academia	22.22	38.89	27.78	11.11
Others	34.62	11.54	26.92	26.92
Average	37.90	26.73	23.42	11.94

Sino-American Trade

The trade controversy has been one of the major issues in Sino-American relations in recent years. China's WTO membership and high growth rate have resulted in rapid expansion of U.S.-China trade and U.S. investment in China. U.S. trade deficits with China have also increased quickly. In fact, China has become the country with which the United States has its largest trade deficit. The unbalanced bilateral trade has drawn public attention in the United States. That the United States blames China for the trade deficit also provokes Chinese to think about this issue.

The survey focused on Chinese views of the trade deficit and of the growing number of U.S. products on the Chinese market. Results show that a plurality believed that the United States blaming China for the

Table 10. Question: In your opinion, what are the motives behind America's policy toward Taiwan?

Respondents	Create obstacles to prevent China from rising	Facilitate territorial ambitions for Taiwan and attempt to turn it into America's unsinkable aircraft carrier in Asia	Fulfill America's international obligation and protect U.S. interests in the Asia-Pacific	Support Taiwan's demo-cratization and promote peaceful evolution in mainland China
Journalists	20.68	15.51	46.55	22.41
College students	30.63	31.65	24.30	13.42
Government officials	36.87	21.21	24.24	17.68
Business-people	31.33	23.33	37.33	8.00
People from academia	38.89	22.22	22.22	16.67
Others	23.08	61.54	11.54	3.85
Average	30.33	26.09	29.68	14.74

deficit stems from strategic considerations; pressures from U.S. business and trade protectionists ranked second, followed by an effort to pressure China to buy more U.S. products. Only a minority of respondents saw America as trying to change China's political system through economic exchange. Some respondents chose more than one answer (table 11).

A plurality welcomed more U.S. products on the Chinese market. Many do not care about the origin of products as long as they are of good quality. Few showed a dislike for U.S. products or thought they are more trustworthy. The answers to this question are consistent in all groups, indicating that Chinese consumers are open to foreign products. Some respondents chose more than one answer (table 12).

Table 11. Question: America has made many accusations in its trade frictions with China. In your opinion, what is the goal of the U.S. government regarding trade?

Respondents	Pressure China to buy more U.S. products and thereby gain more economic benefits	Contain China's growth because of strategic considerations	Placate U.S. business and trade protectionists in a domestic political game to get more votes	Change China's political system through economic exchanges
Journalists	32.75	31.03	29.31	22.41
College students	14.25	47.07	33.08	5.60
Government officials	14.50	59.00	14.50	12.00
Business-people	32.43	39.19	20.95	7.43
People from academia	16.67	27.78	33.33	22.22
Others	7.69	61.54	15.38	15.38
Average	21.10	45.72	26.38	10.63

CONCLUSIONS

This survey provides a lens through which to look at Chinese views of America since 9/11. We have tried to determine, after comparing our results with those of 2000 and 2001 surveys, what has changed—and what has not—since the 9/11 attacks, the U.S. wars in Afghanistan and Iraq, the Korean nuclear crisis, and other international developments. We also sought to identify new trends and deepen our understanding of how Chinese people perceive America. We reached several conclusions.

The love-hate ambivalence that characterizes Chinese views of America has not changed since 9/11. This is consistent with previous findings that the Chinese public separates U.S. domestic policy from its foreign policy. The love is for America's domestic political, economic, and cultural achievements, while the hate is for America's arrogance and overbearing attitude in international affairs.

Table 12. Question: U.S. products and investment in China are increasing. How do you feel about it?

Respondents	It's welcome; an inevitable result of globalization and both countries benefit	I don't like it; it undermines China's national industry and exploits Chinese people	Compared with other imports, U.S. products are of better quality and taste, and U.S. companies are more trustworthy	It doesn't matter which country products are from as long as quality and service are good
Journalists	58.62	0.00	3.44	41.37
College students	40.55	7.56	3.27	48.61
Government officials	50.49	4.90	1.96	42.65
Business-people	46.67	5.33	4.00	44.00
People from academia	50.00	5.56	0.00	44.44
Others	26.92	11.54	0.00	61.54
Average	46.46	5.45	2.73	45.68

Chinese people distinguish the American people from the U.S. administration. Overwhelming majorities had favorable impressions of Americans as warm, open, and accessible; only 1.31 percent thought otherwise. This finding is further confirmed by surveys conducted by other agencies. In 1998, for example, the China Mainland Marketing Research Company polled people on the streets of Beijing, Shanghai, and seven other big cities on their opinions on President Clinton's visit to China. One-third of the people polled said they had an unfavorable view of the U.S. role in international affairs, and 38.2 percent believed the United States was seeking world dominance. A 1997 survey conducted by the Public Opinion Institute at Chinese People's University showed that Chinese people view Americans more favorably than they view Germans, Japanese, and Russians. Americans were considered to make better neighbors, colleagues, and friends.

To the question about whether the United States was on the decline, more people agreed in the latest survey than agreed in earlier surveys. In the 2000 survey, 69 percent thought the United States was not on the decline; 8 percent thought it was. Many respondents wrote that America was in fact becoming more powerful. In the latest survey, 48.88 percent thought that U.S. strength is temporary, that it has become more isolated and that its global influence is in decline; 33.68 percent still believe that America will continue to be prosperous and be the only superpower for a long time to come.

The theory of a China threat overshadows Chinese views of America. There has been a consistent Chinese suspicion about the true intention behind Washington's China policy. U.S. criticism of China's human rights practices, arms sales to Taiwan, trade frictions, the bombing of Chinese embassy in 1999, and the air collision in 2001 all helped solidify this suspicion. 9/11 had little effect.

Taiwan has always been a sensitive issue. Trade frictions have intensified as the U.S. deficit with China has increased. Survey respondents link U.S. intentions on both Taiwan and trade to an effort to contain China's rise.

As in 2000, the latest survey also showed that more people are optimistic about the future of Sino-American relations, believing that the relations will steadily develop and improve. Note, however, that the percentage of those who predict an upcoming conflict between China and the United States rose from 13 percent in 2000 to 23 percent in 2004.

Both surveys found that majorities believe that the United States is more responsible than China for problems between the two countries because they believe that the United States seeks to contain China. In the 2000 survey, 68.94 percent believed the United States was trying to prevent China from becoming a big power. In the latest survey, 30 percent believed that America's Taiwan policy is to create obstacles in China's rising; 45.72 percent believed that U.S. accusations over the trade deficit with China are to contain China's growth out of strategic considerations. When asked to predict the future of U.S.-China relations, 37.90 percent said they believe there will be problems but that a gradual improvement will take place; but 23.42 percent believe the United States will not allow China to become a big power, so there will be serious conflicts in the future.

Compared with the 2000 survey, more 2004 respondents expressed a willingness to know more about the United States. This is probably not in response to 9/11; instead, it is the result of the growing exchanges between China and the United States in recent years.

In the 2000 survey, answers to the question, "How much do you think you know about America?" varied according to respondents' professions and educational levels. Fifty-seven percent of journalists, 34.7 percent of government officials, 23 percent of businesspeople, and 18 percent of college students said they knew something; while 31 percent of journalists, 30 percent of officials, 53.8 percent of businesspeople, and 63 percent of students answered that they knew very little. In the 2004 survey, most respondents said they had some knowledge of, and interest in, U.S. domestic politics. The answer is consistent in all groups and is not affected by group identities.

A new finding in the 2004 survey was that a majority of respondents holds a favorable and open attitude toward U.S. products and culture, even though these respondents also believe that Chinese culture is closer to their lives.

In conclusion, the 2004 survey suggested that the increasing economic, cultural, and personal exchanges between China and the United States have given the Chinese public better access to more sources of information about the United States. As a result, Chinese understanding of the United States has become more sophisticated and more rational, although misunderstanding persists. Chinese images of the United States are complex and diverse. They have undergone some changes since 9/11, but many have stayed the same. More dialogue and exchanges, more balanced media coverage, good textbooks, and a better understanding of each other's history and the current challenges each faces are the best means to build a stable and constructive relationship.

Notes

1. The survey questionnaire in this report was framed by Wang Jisi, director of IAS. Dr. Zhao Xinshu, Dr. Chen Shengluo, and Hu Guocheng, deputy director of

IAS, offered their valuable suggestions to the revision and framing of the questionnaire. It is impossible to mention everyone who participated in the survey. We want to give special thanks to Chen Shengluo, associate professor, China Youth University for Political Science; Sun Zhe, professor, Center for American Studies, Fudan University; Zuo Fengrong, professor, School of the Central Party School; Li Xiaoping, executive producer, assignment desk, CCTV International, China Central Television; Ding Xinghao, director, Shanghai Institute of American Studies; Tang Xiaosong, associate professor, Guangdong University of Foreign Studies; and Zhao Xinshu, associate professor, School of Journalism and Mass Communication, University of North Carolina. They helped conduct surveys in different regions. Dr. Chen Shengluo and Dr. Tang Xiaosong also helped tally the final statistics. Without their enthusiastic support, this project would not have been accomplished. I am grateful to all of them.

2. Paul Kennedy, *The Rise and Fall of the Great Powers: Economic Change and Military Conflict from 1500 to 2000* (New York: Vintage Books, 1989).

3. John J. Mearsheimer, *The Tragedy of Great Power Politics* (New York: Norton, 2001).

CHAPTER SEVEN

CHINESE MEDIA PROFESSIONALS' VIEWS OF AMERICA

Li Xiaoping

THE IMAGE OF THE UNITED STATES in the Chinese media consists of two parts: first, Chinese reporting and programming; and, second, views of Chinese media professionals. This chapter explores through personal interviews, symposia, studies, and observations during my long experience as a journalist how Chinese media professionals see the United States.

Thirty media professionals allowed me to interview them or attended a symposium on this topic. They included journalists and editors from Xinhua News Agency, China Central Television, *Guangming Daily, Global Times*, China News Service, 21st Century Economic Reporting, and *Huangsheng Daily*. All have bachelor's or master's degrees, and they ranged in age:

Journalists' ages	21–5	26–30	31–5	36–40	41–5	46–50	51–5	56–60	60+
Number interviewed	2	9	2	7	2	4	3	0	1

This chapter summarizes these media professionals' opinions and how they became informed about the United States; it also compares them with Chinese from other walks of life. Included are analyses of their views on America, Sino-American relations, Chinese media reporting on the United States, and relations between the government and the media.

CHARACTERISTICS OF MEDIA PROFESSIONALS

Compared with other groups in China, people in the media have more opportunities to learn about and understand the United States and Americans.

First, they get to know the United States by watching American movies, reading American newspapers, and watching American television. People who work in television prefer to watch CNN, for example. They often draw on the U.S. media for research, particularly on issues related to international relations, and are therefore familiar with how the U.S. press covers stories. Meanwhile, they also follow reporting on the United States by Asian, European, and Middle Eastern countries, so they are familiar with how other nations view America. This helps them to get to know and evaluate the United States and to examine their own analysis and opinions.

Chinese media professionals also have more opportunities to go abroad. Of the interviewees and those who attended the symposium, 20 have worked abroad, including 15 who had worked in the United States. While in the United States, they formed a picture of the United States on the basis of direct contact with the people. They have frequent contact with Americans, through whom they understand the United States. Some have also been to other developed nations such as Japan or countries in Europe, providing them a point of comparison. One interviewee commented, "From American movies and the reporting of America, I thought it was a disorderly, murder-prone society without public security. Only after I visited the United States twice did I realize that the reality is a great departure from what I had imagined."

Some of the interviewees learned about the United States directly from American journalists. Six of them had experience working with American journalists or have had contact with them.

Media professionals' experiences make them critical thinkers. Instead of being passive information receivers, media professionals clearly have their own views on and concerns about issues other than their opinions of America. The following views on China-U.S. relations and thoughts on the traditional cultures of the two countries became apparent during interviews with media professionals.

Some of those interviewed believed that many people in the U.S. government have a negative view of China and are afraid of a rising China. The United States is often looking for a "pretend enemy." These media professionals have a strong aversion to the increasing influence of U.S. values on Chinese youth. For example, they do not like the U.S. view that "winners make history," a belief that puts power above morality and principles. In addition, they are uncomfortable with certain ideas reflected in American movies: the United States is unconquerable; American citizens are entitled to privileges; and Americans are infallible. These beliefs and those of big-power chauvinism have an impact on Chinese youngsters to varying degrees.

Others believed that the attitude of the Chinese media and public toward the United States is sentimental and lacks rational analysis. John King Fairbank's *The United States and China* offered a relatively rational approach in helping Americans understand China.[1] Today, the Chinese, too, should adopt a rational attitude toward the United States. Sino-U.S. relations have a heavy historical burden and, from time to time, China is afflicted by the "victim syndrome." On the other hand, Americans should try to understand the Chinese better and put themselves in their shoes.

Still another interviewee believed that U.S. pressure on China has, on some occasions, accelerated China's social progress and serves as a galvanizing factor, as in the case of China's management of the SARS epidemic.

Interviewees also spoke of the differences between the Chinese and the U.S. cultures. Chinese culture is fairly introspective. It prizes the concept of harmony, advocates individual pursuit of personal perfection, and rejects interference in other people's affairs. Since ancient times, the Chinese ruling classes (emperors) preferred using the edifying effect of education in ruling the people rather than force. In contrast, the United States is a young nation, full of creativity and passion, and infused with an enterprising spirit. American culture emphasizes expansion of power and the love of adventure. Therefore, the American way of thinking is more akin to Roman-style heroism. One interviewee commented:

The Chinese and American cultures are complementary by nature. If handled properly, the two may become very good partners and play a positive role in promoting world peace and stability. The United States should give up its efforts to alienate and weaken China [and should not] see China as its rival or enemy.

Others, however, maintained that confrontation between the two countries is inevitable in the future. U.S. foreign policy is developed on the basis of national interest, ideology, and domestic politics. For its part, China will never forsake its national interest in decisionmaking. At present and in the foreseeable future, China and the United States will possess shared interests as well as conflicts. Currently in the United States, the mainstream view of China is that of a potential rival, and many seek to contain China. The United States is not likely to treat a country with such a different social system and ideology on an equal footing. Many Chinese believe that the United States will be friendly with China only when the two countries have shared interests or when the United States needs help from China. Otherwise, the United States finds it difficult to treat China fairly.

MEDIA PROFESSIONALS' VIEWS ABOUT THE UNITED STATES

From February 25, 2004, to April 9, 2004, I interviewed 21 media professionals in Beijing and invited nine journalists and editors from Beijing to a symposium to discuss America's image among media professionals, the Chinese media's reporting on America, and other related topics. The following issues are ranked in the order of most to least attention paid by these journalists.

View of America in General

Fifteen interviewees said their impressions of America were mixed. On the one hand, they like the openness, civil society, democracy, and legal system in the United States. They said the United States is a great nation. With a history of just over 200 years, it has grown into a prosperous, affluent, and developed country, which speaks well of the civilization and the legal system in U.S. society. At the same time, the

United States is a very powerful country. It is also an immigrant nation with a strong sense of assimilation. In the United States, different ethnic and cultural groups get along well with each another, and everyone has equal opportunity. One of the interviewees said, "I identify with the values in America and agree with its respect for humanity, solicitude for individuals, conception of human rights, and regard for the environment, etc."

On the other hand, the interviewees were opposed to U.S. foreign policy and the way it forces its values upon others. They said the United States uses power politics and hegemony, and it interferes in the domestic affairs of other countries. Furthermore, they feel that U.S. foreign policy discriminates against developing countries. Some of the interviewees used terms like "arbitrariness" and "international policeman" when they talked about America. In their opinion, there is not another country to balance U.S. power on the world stage. Furthermore, the United States is unrestrained by a sense of morality and justice.

Interviewees also commented that the United States is unprincipled in the international sphere and said that it is unacceptable that the United States always pushes others to follow its values. For example, with regard to the war in Iraq, one respondent noted, "We disagree with America's deed, which disregards international law, but we do not sympathize with Saddam." Another journalist commented, "I have complex feelings toward September 11. From the viewpoint of humanity, I oppose terrorists who killed the innocent, but I do think such deeds punish America. Why do the Islamic countries resort to such vicious practice? Because they don't have other choices."

Two of the interviewees agreed that U.S. foreign policy has some positive impact on international affairs; at the same time they criticized U.S. arbitrariness. One noted:

> The United States has contributed a lot to the peace and development of the world, especially during and after the Second World War. During the Cold War, the world was controlled by two superpowers. The United States was a crucial counterpower to the Soviet Union, to keeping the world stable and avoiding another world war. American foreign policy was very sophisticated, both in theory and in practice. It was purposive and coherent and more mature than that of any other country. But, on the other

hand, America is surely very arbitrary, following the law of the jungle. American domestic policies are very different from foreign policies. The former is democratic, but the latter is not. The American people respect each other, but the American government is too arrogant in its foreign affairs. There is nothing wrong for a country to pursue its national interest openly, but it should not neglect other countries' interests and hurt others' feelings. America has two totally different criteria in dealing with Israel and the Arabic world. This hardly sounds persuasive to the rest of the world.

Another interviewee described the American image in his mind as positive. He sees America as a decent place. He said America is nice and open. He said he feels at home walking in the streets in America, and he seldom feels like a stranger.

In contrast, two interviewees said their views toward America are mainly negative. The Iraq War disappointed many young people, causing them to no longer trust the United States. Although the United States advocates democracy, it does not behave democratically in the UN and in international affairs. Its power politics and unilateral diplomacy are unconstrained. The United States pursues its national interests in the name of democracy. This deceives people in other countries and makes them feel as if the United States is not a peace-loving nation. The United States is arbitrary in its punishment of countries that do not follow its lead. It also launched wars—wars that have killed many civilians in Kosovo and Iraq—which have cast doubt on America's argument that these wars were in the pursuit of human rights. Because no force can counter U.S. power, the United States totally disregards the opinions of other countries and, for example, is now unpopular among other UN members. Many Americans living or traveling abroad feel ashamed of what their government has done.

View of American People

Many interviewees said that Americans are great people. They are ebullient, diligent, serious, and devoted to their work. America's development is rooted in its people's hard work. The passion of the American people generally makes it easy to communicate with them. Many American people are rather idealistic and simple. Despite advocating diversity on many issues, their basic values are surprisingly similar. They have deep-rooted preconceptions about other countries, especially those with ideologies or social systems different from their own.

At the same time, several interviewees said they were astonished by Americans' ignorance about other countries. While living in the most advanced information society in the world, they have little knowledge about international affairs. One interviewee talked about his experience in the United States: he was standing in a line for a meal at Cable News Network (CNN) and found the conversations around him thought provoking: "Where are you from?" "From South Africa." "Are you still fighting for Lebanon?" "Where are you from?" "From Spain." "What language do you speak?"

That said, most of the interviewees expected China to learn from America's development experience as a point of reference. The following quote from a Chinese scholar captures the mentality of most Chinese media professionals: "Chinese people made America the model of China. They hoped that with great efforts, China could one day become as rich, as powerful, and as unique as today's United States."[2]

View of American Media

Many Chinese media professionals admit that they often refer to American media for information because a large part of the global information flow originates in the United States. Such news is infused with U.S. views and reflects U.S. attitudes toward developing countries. They believe that CNN is selective in its reporting. One journalist said that, when she was at CNN, journalists from the Middle East said CNN's reporting on the Middle East was biased and that those doing the reporting knew little about the Middle East. Furthermore, she felt they did not want to know the realities of the places from which they were reporting. Similarly, interviewees found that U.S. media reporting about China was also unbalanced. Chinese media professionals feel that the U.S. media always focuses on the trifling and seamy side of China.

Before the June 4, 1989, Tiananmen incident, U.S. media reported little about China. Recently, however, the United States has changed its attitude toward China because of China's economic development and its increasing power.

Several interviewees have had an opportunity to work with journalists from the U.S. media. They said American journalists usually prejudge an issue before they investigate it; they then conduct their reporting according to their prejudices. One interviewee said he had been to Xinjiang with an American journalist from CNN. Both journalists interviewed the same people in the same mosques, but their reporting turned out very differently. The CNN journalist was interested only in issues of religious freedom and whether local ethnic minorities were losing their traditions and culture.

Another interviewee had spoken with several American journalists who work in Beijing. She commented:

> Their devotion to their work and their professionalism are very admirable. Some of them know a lot about China. They say China is energetic and is developing quickly. Chinese people are ebullient and easy to talk to. But some other American journalists seem to be aloof to the developments of China while enthusiastically pursuing topics they hold to be valuable, such as stories about dissenters and human rights. They believe some American editors ask their journalists in Beijing to report on issues like Falungong, dissent, Tibet and Xinjiang independence movements, and human rights. And if they do not, their reports will be shelved or cut. If this is the case, then American news values about China are biased. They don't know China, and they don't want to know China. Their only interest is in ideology.
>
> I visited Vietnam last year with some journalists from other Asian countries and the United States. Vietnam is a war-ravaged country. What journalists from Asian countries (including me) wanted to know and paid most attention to was how the country was coping with the aftermath of the war; whether there was enough food for ordinary local people; how many people still live in poverty; what the current situation is with the land mines; and how the war is still affecting people. However, American journalists had little interests in these topics. They asked three questions repeatedly: whether there is freedom of the press; whether there is religious freedom; and what this country could do for America. Most of my Asian colleagues found this lamentable—it showed they care only about themselves but care little for people in other countries. Their attitude about human rights is deceptive. They have never had to struggle just to survive, so they do not understand that human rights for many people of Vietnam is simply having something to eat.

Attitude toward American Culture

Most interviewees under the age of 40 said they accept, welcome, and appreciate American culture. They like American culture for its openness and liveliness. They said that American culture is easy to understand and is imbued with a feeling of freedom. Overall, American culture is well received.

Most media professionals who have been to the United States are impressed by its vast and open territory and abundant resources. Its living conditions and natural environment are superior. People in America are very close to nature, which nurtures their passion for life. Given the balance of its resources and population, the U.S. standard of living compares favorably even to that of Europe in many aspects. The natural resources in Europe have largely been depleted, but the United States enjoys many advantages and has a lot of potential for further development.

Summary of Media Professionals' Views

Chinese media professionals evaluate the United States mainly according to its ethics. They love the United States and the American people because they think America's democracy, civil society, and values are righteous and moral. However, they detest U.S. foreign policy because, in their opinion, the United States is unprincipled in international affairs and its human rights arguments are hypocritical. They are also critical of the U.S. media, which is, in their view, not objective and does not live up to their own standards.

America is something of a "perfect country" in the opinion of Chinese media professionals who have been to the United States. They think America's political and social systems, its values, its vast territory, and its abundant resources are perfect. They hope that China can be as democratic, developed, and prosperous as America, and they hope to use America as the model for China's development. They have high expectations of America.

To interviewees who have not been to the United States, it is a remote and strange country. They do not have a developed image of America and their knowledge about it is somewhat random and unsystematic because they have not spent much time studying U.S. history, politics, or society. They are practical, and they evaluate the United States according to traditional Chinese values and current Chinese interests. They do not really care about domestic U.S. affairs and do not pay much attention to U.S. political events such as the recent presidential election. They are mainly concerned about issues related to China's interests, such as Sino-American relations, China becoming a member of the WTO, and conflicts in Sino-American trade, among others.

Younger interviewees (under the age of 35), especially those who have never been to the United States, are ambivalent about America. Sometimes they admire America but other times they hate it. Their image of America is somewhat inconsistent and is easily affected by current events. One interviewee noted:

> I admired America very much when I was still a college student, feeling that America's democracy was perfect and its economy so powerful. Despite its short history, American culture is addictive. Many Chinese people admired America, imagining it was paradise-like, a perfect country. All until America's unlawful inspection of the Chinese cargo ship *Galaxy* on July 23, 1993, which insulted China. Then the bombing of the Chinese embassy in Belgrade and the collision of the American EP-3 surveillance plane with a Chinese fighter jet over the South China Sea turned America into an evil country to us.

Interviewees 36 and older tend to have a more consistent opinion about the United States. They detest its foreign policy, power politics, double standards, and arrogance; however, they also have a clear perception of the common interests of the United States and China. Their different experiences, coupled with their own observations over the years, make their views less susceptible to events.

ASSESSMENT

Chinese Media Coverage Now More Balanced

A majority of the interviewees believed that compared with two or three decades ago, during the early stage of reform and opening up, Chinese media coverage of the United States has become more objective and balanced, although sometimes it still reveals remnants of Cold War thinking. In the 1980s, for example, one could still read stories in China about homeless people in the United States roaming the streets at Christmas. The story might have been accompanied by a picture of an old, homeless man warming himself beside a subway vent, with the backdrop of brightly lit streets and glittering Christmas trees. It is unlikely, however, that such a story would be printed in Chinese newspapers today. Even if a journalist possesses such an article or photograph, the editors would not allow them to be published, for it is well known that this does not portray the reality of average life in the United States.

Many interviewees believed that coverage of the United States takes priority over all other international news reporting. The volume of reporting is large, and coverage is quite balanced. This view to some extent tracks with the conclusions of a 2002 University of Maryland report, "Perspectives toward the United States in Selected Newspapers of the People's Republic of China," which states: "Chinese reporting on the U.S. appears to be relatively balanced overall. . . . We found a current tendency toward generally objective reporting."[3] More balanced reporting on the United States is the result of deeper understanding of the United States by Chinese media professionals.

Chinese media reporting on the United States remains selective, however. Apart from regular news and breaking news coverage, much reporting reflects media professionals' concerns over domestic affairs. Chinese media professionals have a strong sense of social responsibility. Over the years, they have introduced their domestic viewers and readers to an array of information regarding the U.S. experience that has proved helpful in the social and economic development of China. They hope that such reporting will propel China's development and help China solve its own problems.

Several interviewees commented that currently the coverage in China of the United States is more positive than negative, which has the effect of "beautifying" the United States. One reporter recalled that his past reporting on U.S. multinationals later turned out to be quite biased in favor of the U.S. companies. On the one hand, this betrays the fact that Chinese media professionals still lack a comprehensive understanding of the United States. More often than not, they are able to observe only the surface of U.S. society, and they do not go deeper. On the other hand, there is a problem of media professionals' idealizing the United States.

The Chinese Government and Public Opinion

Several interviewees spoke of reports that used to appear in the U.S. media accusing the Chinese government of stirring up anti-American sentiment among the Chinese public. After the Tiananmen incident, the Chinese government used a number of vehicles to criticize the United States, a practice it later officially stopped.

In fact, it is the Americans, not the Chinese government, who have educated Chinese youth about the United States. The *Yinhe* incident,[4] Lee Teng-hui's 1995 visit to the United States, the 1995–1996 crisis in the Taiwan Strait, the 1999 bombing of Chinese embassy in Belgrade, the 2001 EP-3 incident, and other incidents all left a deep impression on the Chinese people. Chinese youth, especially college students, surf the Internet and can read the U.S. coverage of these events. It is U.S. action and U.S. media coverage of that action that alienate young Chinese.

On the other hand, even when conflicts arise between the two countries, the Chinese media often exercise constraint in their reporting on the United States. China has many domestic problems to tackle, such as dealing with laid-off workers and returning delayed payments to migrant workers. Therefore, the Chinese government hopes to maintain domestic stability and avoid direct confrontation with the United States. For this reason, Chinese authorities hope that the media will emphasize the healthy developments in Sino-U.S. relations.

One American friend recalled that when the EP-3 incident took place, she was in Shanghai and closely followed the Chinese media's coverage of the event. She found that the Chinese media took a sober stand on the incident and did not reveal strong anti-American sentiment, obviously at the instruction of the Chinese government. The American friend said that she was filled with ambivalence. As an American championing news freedom, she is always opposed to government intervention in the media; but, in this instance, the Chinese government intervened in a way that stabilized Sino-U.S. relations and served the U.S. interest.

U.S.-Style Democracy and China

Some media professionals hold up U.S. democracy as a model for China because they believe that democracy is China's only choice for catching up with the United States. Other professionals compare and try to learn from other countries' diverse experiences. They are concerned about political reform and democratization in Russia; they compare politics and democracy in South Korea and the Philippines; and they try to analyze why Singapore and Malaysia choose not to adopt the Western democratic model. The 2004 Taiwan presidential election also serves as an excellent case study for Chinese media professionals.

When they examine the paths that different countries have taken, one of the main questions media professionals ask is, "What conditions suit the nature of Western democracy?" They hold notions of civil society, democracy, and the rule of law in high esteem but at the same time feel that the U.S. system does not always work in other countries, nor does it readily apply to China. One interviewee stated, "America's model cannot be imitated. If carried out in Palestine, most likely the leaders of Hamas will get elected." Another commented, "At present, American-style democracy doesn't fit in with Chinese conditions. The Russian experience is a good lesson. The ideal of democracy can only be realized in China step by step." Another added, "If China pursues Western democracy now, it would result in a farce. The nation would be separated and political corruption would run rampant. The situation in the mainland may be even worse than Taiwan. The general education level of the Chinese still must be raised. Therefore, China at present demands a strong central government."

U.S. Foreign Policy and Public Opinion

A majority of the media professionals criticized U.S. foreign policy: they wondered why the United States is not concerned about strong anti-American feelings around the world. They questioned whether hegemony is in fact in the U.S. interest in the long run. They stated that U.S. foreign policy is formulated by elites who are accountable to neither the international community nor the American public. In early 2004, Susan Shirk, a China expert at the University of California, San

Diego, stated, "In the United States and other democratic countries, foreign policy makers pay little attention to public opinion, unless it is on the eve of an election."[5] The ignorance and indifference of the U.S. public toward international affairs means that public opinion rarely gives rise to strong opposition to U.S. foreign policy; public opinion then becomes de facto acquiescence, or even agreement, with U.S. policy abroad.

Notes

1. John King Fairbank, *The United States and China,* 4th ed. (Cambridge: Harvard University Press, 1979).

2. Niu Jun, "Rise of China: Different Understanding at Home and Abroad," *Global Times,* November 14, 2003.

3. Deborah A. Cai, "Perspectives toward the United States in Selected Newspapers of the People's Republic of China" (College Park: University of Maryland, Institute for Global Chinese Affairs and the Department of Communication, May 30, 2002), pp. 5–6, www.uscc.gov/researchpapers/2000_2003/pdfs/chinmed.pdf.

4. On the basis of U.S. intelligence, in 1993 the United States claimed that a Chinese cargo ship, the *Yinhe* (Galaxy), was carrying chemical weapons to Iran. An inspection found no such weapons, and the incident caused tensions in the U.S.-China bilateral relationship.

5. Susan Shirk, quoted in "Public Opinion and Foreign Policy Making," *Global Times,* January 16, 2004.

CHAPTER EIGHT

RETURNED OVERSEAS CHINESE VIEWS OF AMERICA

Li Xiaogang

In China, a person who has received specialized education or training (at least a university degree) is often called a "talent." According to their educational background, current Chinese talents can be divided into two categories: native talents who went to college in China and have no experience of research abroad, and returned overseas talents who are popularly named *Hai Gui Pai*.[1] Most Chinese returned overseas talents today return from studying in Western developed countries.[2] This is in accordance to the current open-door policy, which in fact means opening to the West.[3]

Returned talents belong to a special group in China. They grew up in China and have personally experienced the state of China. When they were abroad, they were imperceptibly influenced by the science and technology, economy, society, politics, and culture of the host countries—the United States and countries with levels of development and values similar to those of the United States. Almost all returned talents, therefore, have some direct or indirect knowledge of the United States. On the one hand, contemporary Chinese returned overseas talents' images of the United States are the products of exchange and some collision between Chinese and Western cultures. On the other hand, because most of the returned talents now are leaders or professional elites in their respective fields, their images of the United States will influence the further development of Sino-U.S. interaction.

To explore returned talents' perceptions of the United States, we undertook a survey in February–March 2004. The survey was conducted by questionnaire, telephone interviews, and e-mail. We did a random sampling based on the following criteria: the countries in which the returned talents lived and studied; the areas of academic specialization; age; current profession;[4] and geographical location.

Specifically, we surveyed returned talents who had studied in the United States, West European countries, Australia, and Japan. Their specialties included humanities, science and engineering, agriculture, and medicine. They are now scientists, researchers, university professors, and doctors, among other professions. We interviewed not only returned talents who live in East Coast cities such as Beijing, Shanghai, and Guangzhou, but also those who live in southwestern and northwestern cities such as Chongqing, Chengdu, and Xi'an. We grouped interviewees into age ranges: 35–45, 45–60, and 60 and older.

The survey was limited to some extent. First, opinion research is a relatively new science in China. Most of the returned talents interviewed are established and even famous in their respective fields. Some were concerned that the interviews would be used in the media and would affect their personal images. As a result, it is possible that some tried to polish their answers. In addition, because the returned talents are busy professionals, it was sometimes difficult to get detailed answers.

Through the survey, we found that on most issues returned talents' perceptions of the United States have little or nothing to do with their ages, occupations, domiciles, or the countries in which they had studied. The returned talents who had studied in the United States have perceptions of the United States very similar to those who studied in countries that are comparable with the United States in terms of social development, political system, and ideology.

RETURNED OVERSEAS TALENTS AND CONTEMPORARY CHINESE SOCIETY

In 1978, the Chinese government established a basic national policy of reform and an open door. Deng Xiaoping realized that this policy would enable China to build local talent by sending students and scholars abroad to learn Western countries' advanced technology and managerial experience. In June 1978, Deng called for an acceleration of this effort:

> We must enlarge the number of students to study abroad, we should send out tens of thousands of them, not just ten or eight students. . . . Choose three or four thousand students this year, send out ten thousand next year . . . . The Department of Education must pay much attention to this issue. It will be worthy no matter how much money has to be spent.[5]

Because of Deng's personal involvement, sending students abroad became an important task for the Chinese government, and the United States responded positively. In September 1978, the two governments signed an agreement for education exchanges. One year later, China reached agreement on education exchange with Great Britain, Canada, and the Netherlands and, in 1980, signed similar agreements with Japan, Germany, France, and Belgium.

In October 1978, the first group—50 Chinese students—to study abroad in the reform-and-open-door period arrived in the United States and entered universities. Since then, the number of Chinese students or scholars who have studied abroad has totaled approximately 700,200.[6] In 2003 alone, approximately 117,000 Chinese students went abroad, more than one-third to the United States. Of the total number of students or scholars who have studied abroad, 172,800 have returned to China and 356,600 are still studying in foreign universities or working as visiting scholars. In recent years, students and scholars returning to China have increased by 13–15 percent per year. In 2003, 20,100 Chinese students returned to China, the first time that the number of returning students exceeded 20,000 in any one year.[7]

By studying abroad, students and scholars have enlarged their scope of research, learned about developed countries' scientific research techniques and trends, improved their research capabilities, and built academic exchange channels. After returning to China, these talents gradually become the backbone of fields such as scientific research, education, economy, trade, medicine, and management. According to official statistics, 81 percent of the academics at the Chinese Academy of Sciences, 54 percent of academics at the Chinese Academy of Engineering, 72 percent of the chief scientists of the "National Program of 863" in the ninth Five-Year Plan, 62.31 percent of Ph.D. candidate tutors, 77.61 percent of presidents of universities directly led by the Ministry of Education, and 94 percent of the directors of the scientific and research institutes have studied abroad.[8]

In business and economics, the Ministry of Education, Ministry of Science and Technology, Ministry of Personnel, and the Bureau of Foreign Experts established 21 "National-Classed Enterprise Gardens for Returned Overseas Talents." The returned talents have established more than 5,000 enterprises with an output value of more than 30 billion renminbi (RMB) ($3.6 million).[9] By September 2002, 1,357 enterprises were in the Zhongguancun Science and Technology Garden; 34.5 percent of the founders are returned doctors, and 48.4 percent have foreign master's degrees. Today, there are about 4,000 returned talents in the garden, and approximately two *Hai Gui Pai* enterprises are founded daily. Shanghai attracts more returned talents than any other city in China. By September 2002, returned talents had established nearly 2,000 enterprises in Shanghai, attracting more than 30,000 returned talents.[10]

Since the early 1990s, returned talents have increasingly entered government service and have become essential officials. In 1993, for example, Wei Yu, who received a Ph.D. in Germany, was appointed deputy commissioner of the National Education Commission. She was the first returned talent to hold a ministerial position in the central government. Since then, the number of returned talents holding ministerial positions has gradually increased, and many returned talents have become bureau heads. For example, Zhou Ji, the present minister of education, received his master's and doctoral degrees from the State University of New York. Before taking on his current post, he served as mayor of Wuhan, the capital city of Hubei province. Chen Zhili, a state councilor, was a visiting scholar at the University of Pennsylvania for two years. Xu Guanhua, minister of science and technology, was a visiting scholar in Sweden. Ma Songde, deputy minister of science and technology, studied in France. Cheng Jinpei, another deputy minister, graduated from Northwestern University near Chicago. Suo Lisheng, deputy minister of the department of water conservancy, received his

Ph.D. from the University of Michigan.[11] In January 2002, the China Development Research Center of the State Council signed an agreement with the John F. Kennedy School of Government at Harvard University, under which China will send 60 central government bureau-level or local government mayor-level officials to study in the United States every year. This agreement will further increase the number of returned talents in various levels of government.

More and more returned overseas talents have become leaders of local governments. For example, Ge Honglin, the mayor of Chengdu, was a visiting scholar in Canada. Returned overseas talents—such as Li Qun, party secretary of Linyi, Shandong Province, and Li Yuguan, deputy mayor of Foshan, Guangdong Province—are playing important roles in lower-level governments as well. In December 2001, the Liaoning provincial government opened 118 head-of-county positions and publicly welcomed returned talents to compete for them. Recently, more than 200 returned overseas talents have joined the Shanghai government every year. At the end of April 2002, a delegation from Shanghai's Pudong District went to San Francisco, Toronto, and Boston to recruit Chinese talents. The slogan of the delegation was *"Hai Gui Pai* can become *Chuzhang."*[12]

Returned talents have always been the initiators and founders of contemporary Chinese humanities and sciences, and they have also influenced Chinese politics. At the beginning of twentieth century, the Chinese government and public regarded Japan as a model of modernization. During this period, about 50,000 students went to Japan to study. In 1905, the members of Tongmeng Hui (founded by Sun Zhongshan [Sun Yat-sen]) were all Chinese students who had studied in Japan. Of the 12 cabinet members of the provisional government of the Republic of China, founded in 1912, eight were returned talents. Sun, the father of the Kuomintang and founder of the ROC, had years of experience of investigation and revolutionary activities in Japan and the United States. His successor, Jiang Jieshi, had also studied in Japan. After 1915, the trend for Chinese students was to go to France for work-study programs (*Qin Gong Jian Xue*), and before 1920 about 1,600 young people went to France. In July 1921, when the CCP was founded, 8 of the 12 delegates who attended the first party congress had studied abroad. Zhou Enlai, Deng Xiaoping, Chen Yi, Nie Rongzhen, and Li Fuchun, among other Chinese Communist leaders, all studied in France. Deng became the core of the leading group of the second generation of the CCP.

In the 1950s and 1960s, 17,000 students and scholars were sent to the Soviet Union and East European countries, and they all returned to China. Among them, Jiang Zemin, Li Peng, Li Lanqing, Wei Jianxing, Zou Jiahua, Liu Huaqing, and Cao Gangchuan later emerged as national leaders. Jiang became the core of the third generation of party leadership. Based on China's history, we can surely anticipate that the 170,000 returned overseas talents from the United States and other developed countries since the beginning of reform and the open door will influence China's future development. As a result, how these people perceived the United States will directly or indirectly influence China's foreign policy.

General Perceptions of the United States

According to the survey, returned talents appear to have a very positive image of the American people. Eighty-four percent of interviewees[13] expressed the view that Americans are, compared with other peoples, warm-hearted, polite, generous, happy to help others, and easy to get to know. One Chinese scholar recounted that, after he had had a traffic accident, his landlord and landlady took care of him, helped him with medical subsidies, and helped him find a lawyer to ask about compensation issues. Others reported that Americans helped them feel less lonely and more relaxed when they first arrived in the United States. About 10 percent said, however, that although they have a generally positive image of American people, they also think that Americans do not care about other people's interests and feelings. Another 10 percent said that there are not obvious differences between Americans and people from other developed countries.

Returned talents also have a generally positive image of the United States. Fifty-seven percent of interviewees said they view the United States positively; they cited its advanced economy and science and its well-run legal system. One scholar said with deep feeling: "The consciousness of American government officials is to serve the public and to strictly observe disciplines. The American people's legal and moral consciousness has deeply impressed me."

Some of the interviewees stressed the stability of the U.S. social system. Thirty-two percent commented that they have both positive and negative impressions of the United States. Domestically, the U.S. political system is run well, the social order is stable, and its people are satisfied with their jobs and lives. At the same time, there are problems such as racial issues, the widening gap between the rich and the poor, and U.S. foreign policy, especially toward China. Six percent believe that the United States was too complicated to truly understand. No one had a completely negative image of the United States, although 5 percent refused to answer this question.

The returned talents' images of the United States are related to whether they hope their children will go to the United States to study or work in the future. Twenty-three percent said that, if their children have the opportunity to study in the United States, they will strongly encourage them to do so. Seventy-one percent expressed hope that their children will be able to study in the United States, but they noted that this decision will be made on the basis of financial support and the specialty their children plan to study. Six percent did not answer this question.

On the issue of U.S. status in the world and its future development, 64 percent stated that the United States will continue its economic prosperity and maintain its sole-superpower status for a considerable period. Nine percent disagreed, arguing that the status of the United States is starting to decline. Fourteen percent expressed the view that America's powerful status is temporary, and it is becoming increasingly isolated in the world. Thirteen percent suggested that America's future will depend on whether the United States continues to pursue its current policy of unilateralism and hegemony internationally; domestically, U.S. development will depend on whether the United States will continue its current post–September 11, 2001, xenophobic policy, particularly its exclusionary immigration and visa policies, and on whether U.S. racial problems continue to increase.

Images of U.S. Domestic Politics

Sixty-four percent of interviewees are interested in and know a little about U.S. domestic politics; 19 percent are not interested and are unwilling to learn; and 17 percent think it is very difficult to understand U.S. politics because of the huge differences in U.S. and Chinese domestic politics. Interviewees attitudes are influenced by choice of occupation and place of study. Those who work in the fields of humanities and arts are generally interested in and know a little about U.S. politics. Those who studied in Japan and those who are working in the fields of science and technology, agriculture, and medicine are less concerned with and know less about U.S. politics.

On the question of democracy in the United States and the market economy, returned oversea talents largely agree. Eighty-nine percent believe that the U.S. system has brought prosperity and stability to the United States but that this does not mean that the U.S. system is applicable to developing countries. Most interviewees held that societies in different stages of development need different rules and systems. The developing countries need to learn something from the United States, but they cannot simply import the U.S. system to their own societies. One of the returned talents said, "At present, China is moving to accept American rules. This is like an operation. Even though we can transplant another person's arm or leg to our own body, we are not sure we can move them at our will." However, he optimistically pointed out that the thinking style of the Chinese people is going to change as the whole society changes, and Chinese people will gradually learn to "use the arms and legs that are transplanted from other bodies." Six percent of interviewees—most of whom had returned from Europe or are working in the arts—believe that the level of development in the United States is not as high as in some Western European countries such as France and Germany. Five percent did not answer this question.

Fifty-one percent think that the United States has created many valuable cultural products. Thirty-three percent think these products are acceptable, but they like the cultural products that have Chinese characteristics much more. Eight percent do not like U.S. cultural products because they see these products as biased. Another 8 percent think that U.S. cultural products are vulgar, overly commercial, and not as good as European and Chinese cultural products. Age and occupation influenced interviewees' attitudes: those who like U.S. cultural products are either between 35 and 45 years of age or are working in the fields of humanities and social sciences. Most people who are older than 45 prefer Chinese cultural products.

Images of U.S. Foreign Policy

Most interviewees think that the United States uses its power to behave unilaterally and as a hegemon. On the question about the Iraq War, 56 percent were opposed, and 23 percent described themselves as strongly opposed. Eleven percent of interviewees believe that the decision to go to war was to some degree reasonable, but the way the war has been waged has been wrong. Ten percent believe that the war is none of China's business.

Attitudes toward China-U.S. Relations

Most of the returned talents expressed concern with China-U.S. relations, and, in general, they are not very optimistic about the future of the bilateral relationship. Only 14 percent held a positive attitude. They believe that the people of the two countries will gradually understand each other much better as exchange activities increase. Although there are some contradictions between the two countries, the bilateral relationship will gradually improve. Thirty-one percent believe that the bilateral relationship will remain the status quo, that is, not very good and not very bad, with ups and downs. Nineteen percent are pessimistic about the future. They believe that the United States will not let China develop into a powerful country and that there is a possibility that the two countries will have a conflict. Fourteen percent believe, however, that the United States cannot tolerate any other country's rise, including but not limited to China. If China adopts an appropriate and flexible foreign policy, a conflict with the United States may not be inevitable. Twenty-three percent believe that there is too much uncertainty and it is difficult to make a judgment.

On the question of U.S. policy toward Taiwan, the U.S. government has always claimed that Taiwan represents a successful case of democratization in the Confucian cultural zone and that U.S. support of Taiwan is aimed at protecting democracy. None of the returned talents interviewed believed that the real intention of the United States is to support Taiwan's democracy. On the contrary, 73 percent believed that the U.S. motive is to protect U.S. strategic interests in the Asia-Pacific region. Twenty-seven percent believed that U.S. policy toward Taiwan is designed to prevent China from growing into a powerful country.

China-U.S. economic and trade relations are growing closer and closer. Most of the interviewees are supportive of the exchanges between the two countries. Sixty-six percent believe that increasingly close economic relations are the natural result of globalization and will lead to a win-win outcome for both countries. Twenty-five percent do not care about where the commodities they buy come from, but they do care about the quality. Nine percent think that more U.S. goods and capital are now in China's market, which could challenge China's national industries and make China's economy more vulnerable to the U.S. economy.

Bilateral trade frictions are a hot issue in China. The U.S. government criticizes China's exchange rate and complains about the large trade deficit. Sixty-four percent of the interviewed returned talents believe that this is related to U.S. domestic politics. The U.S. government feels compelled to focus on these issues as a means of gaining political support from companies and other constituency groups. As a matter of fact, the United States also has trade frictions with other Western countries. Nine percent believe that the United States hopes to change China's political system through economic exchanges. Twenty percent believe that the United States wants to press China to purchase more U.S. goods, so that is can make more profits. Seven percent believe that the United States is motivated by a strategic consideration to constrain China's rising power.

CONCLUSIONS

Most returned oversea talents share the same image of the United States. On most issues, no matter the overall impression of the United States or U.S. domestic and foreign policies, the survey shows that most returned overseas talents share common opinions, although there are also some disagreements. On the question of how to view the U.S. status in the world, for example, some believe that the United States is declining or becoming more isolated. Most believe, however, that the United States will continue to be the sole superpower for the foreseeable future. On the question of the bilateral trade frictions between China and the United States, some returned talents think that the more U.S. commodities that come into China's market, the worse Chinese national industries will become. Mainstream opinion among the talents holds that this is a natural result of globalization and that both countries will benefit from expanded trade. In short, the returned talents' prevailing view is neither strong criticism nor extreme admiration of the United States. Because it is likely that returned talents will have considerable influence on Chinese society, this typical view is conducive to maintaining a stable Chinese policy toward the United States.

Ideology is fading in importance. No interviewee holds an absolutely negative attitude toward the U.S. social and political systems or believes that the U.S. systems can be transferable to other countries. The consensus is that the U.S. systems have contributed to economic growth and technological development, but other counties, like China, also have their own national conditions. China can learn something from the United States but cannot copy the U.S. experience.

Most returned talents hold a calm attitude toward U.S. critiques of and hostility toward China's ideology. From their point of view, the possibility of ideological conflict between the two countries is declining, and even if such a conflict takes place, it will not be serious enough to have a major impact on the bilateral relationship.

Most support the development of bilateral economic relations and believe that trade frictions are not a big issue. Most interviewees support the development of economic relationships between China and the United States because they hold a positive attitude toward the development of U.S. science, technology, economy, and the process of globalization. With their knowledge of U.S. domestic politics, they can reasonably understand and not overreact to bilateral trade frictions.

China-U.S. relations can be improved further. The relationship between the two countries depends on the mutual impressions of the citizens of both countries. Most returned talents have a very good impression of the American people and a positive evaluation of the stability of the U.S. political system and its highly developed economy and technology. They appreciate U.S. culture and are interested in America's domestic affairs. If possible, they would like to send their children to study in the United States. The overwhelming mainstream opinion among returned talents is, "The United States is an advanced country. It is necessary for China to know about America and gain the knowledge and methods that can help China realize the goal of modernization."[14] Therefore, returned talents believe there is room for further improvement in China-U.S. relations, and they typically support China's current policy toward the United States, which is "develop cooperation, avoid confrontation."

A multipolar world is supported. Returned overseas talents are opposed to a unilateral U.S. foreign policy. They think that the United States does not consider the interests and feelings of other countries. In this respect, they support a multipolar world that checks U.S. strength, constrains its behavior, and reduces its influence. But they do not go to extremes. Their support of a multipolar world situation exists more in their minds; it is not necessarily reflected in their behavior. For example, on the question of the Iraq War, their opposition is mainly demonstrated in their attitudes. A few returned talents signed the "Statement on Opposition to the U.S. Government's War Plan on Iraq" before the war and called upon the Chinese people at home and abroad to oppose U.S. military action and to "participate in the great global antiwar movement." This statement did not receive much response, however, which shows that for most returned talents the multipolarization proposition is more wishful thinking than a practical goal.

When U.S. hegemony harms concrete Chinese interests—the Taiwan issue, for example—most people hold a strong hostility to U.S. foreign policy and regard multipolarization as a necessary objective. They push to build a multipolar world to undercut U.S. hegemony and release the pressure on China. Their attitudes toward China-U.S. relations and the Taiwan issue reflect this view.

Concern exists about the future of China-U.S. relations; the issue of Taiwan is the key problem. The only common disagreement among the returned overseas talents is about the future of China-U.S. relations. Only a few believe that the bilateral relationship will improve. Fifty percent believe that either the bilateral relationship will maintain the status quo or the relationship could worsen and result in conflict. This seems contradictory to the overall positive view of the China-U.S. relationship, but this can be explained by the Taiwan issue. The interviewees are more in agreement on the Taiwan issue than on other questions. Some believe that U.S. support of Taiwan is to maintain its own strategic interests in the Asia-Pacific region, while others believe that the U.S. aim is to constrain China through maintaining the division between Taiwan and the mainland.

In other words, it is the Taiwan issue that makes returned talents suspicious of U.S. strategic intentions. When we were carrying out the survey, the 2004 Taiwan presidential election was also under way. The Taiwan authorities' use of "unification versus independence" as an election tool caused the returned talents to worry about the development of the Taiwan secession movement. Although the mainland has always stressed that it will not give up its goal of peaceful unification, the unbridled development of the Taiwanese secession movement could compel the mainland to use force, which in turn will bring in the United States and set up a military confrontation.

The Taiwan issue clearly has a direct and significant influence on the attitudes of the returned talents toward the United States. They are worried about the future of China-U.S. relations because of uncertainty over this critical issue. This sense of uncertainty is also shared by Shi Yinhong, a professor of international politics, who points out that if tensions over Taiwan get worse, the China-U.S. relationship will be further strained and put at risk.[15] For responsible scholars and politicians, the essential task on the Taiwan issue is just as Wang Jisi has pointed out: If we do not have creative and strategic foresight and cannot create a constructive environment, it is likely that China and the United States will move into a dangerous hostility.[16]

Notes

1. In its narrow sense in China, *Hai Gui Pai* refers only to returned students who received specialized training and a master's or a doctoral degree in the developed countries. In its general meaning, *Hai Gui Pai* also includes visiting scholars. In this chapter, the term "returned overseas talents" has a meaning similar to *Hai Gui Pai* in a general sense and includes both returned overseas students and visiting scholars.

2. In China today, "Western countries" and "developed countries" refer to the same countries. In the past, they were two different terms. Before the current reform and open-door policy, Western countries had a strong ideological meaning. China used this expression to describe politically reactionary developed countries, and, at that time, Western countries was a derogatory term. Since the end of 1970s, China has increasingly used "developed countries" to refer to those economically and scientifically advanced Western countries. Comparatively speaking, "developed countries" has a more positive meaning. In the 1990s, the ideological meaning of "Western countries" faded in China. In today's media, the two terms are generally used interchangeably or even simultaneously; but when political disagreements such as human rights issues are involved, the official media mainly use the term "Western countries." Therefore, the meanings of the two terms are still somewhat different.

3. Before the current policy of reform and an open door, China mainly closed its door to Western countries but was comparatively open to the Third World. This was reflected not only in China's political and economic support to the national liberation movements in Asia, Africa, and Latin America, but also in China's cultural and medical exchanges with countries in those regions.

4. The survey does not include scholars whose jobs are international studies because their focus on and knowledge of the United States are exceptional.

5. "Deng Xiaoping's Instruction on Sending Students Abroad (June 23, 1978)"; see Song Jian, "Bai Nian Jie Li Liu Xue Chao," *Guangming Daily*, April 14, 2003.

6. This figure is accurate through the end of 2003.

7. Ministry of Education press conference on Chinese Students abroad, China Education and Research Network, February 16, 2004, www.cernet.edu.cn/2004 0216/3099067.shtml.

8. Ibid. Also see *Shen Zhou Xue Ren* (electronic journal), February 15, 2004, www.chisa.edu.cn/chisa/column/index/index.xml.

9. Ministry of Education press conference on Chinese Students abroad, China Education and Research Network, February 16, 2004, www.cernet.edu.cn/ 20040216/3099067.shtml.

10. *Zhong Guo Qing Nian Bao* [China youth] (newspaper), October 11, 2002.

11. *Guang Jiao Jing* (newspaper, Hong Kong), December 12, 2003; *Lian He Zao Bao* (newspaper, Singapore), March, 18, 2003. Additional information on Web sites of departments of the State Council.

12. *Guang Jiao Jing,* December 12, 2003; *Lian He Zao Bao,* March, 18, 2003.

13. Although some interviewees had studied in other counties and had not been to the United States, almost all returned talents have met American people at places such as academic meetings, and 60 percent of those who had studied in the United States have had the experience of traveling in other countries. They based their comparisons of Americans and other people on these experiences.

14. Niu Jun, "Misgivings and Apprehension: The Chinese View of the United States," in *China-United States Sustained Dialogue, 1986–2001,* ed. Maxine Thomas and Zhao Mei (Beijing: China Social Science Press [joint project of the Institute of American Studies, Chinese Academy of Social Sciences, and Charles F. Kettering Foundation], 2001), pp. 82–83.

15. Shi Yinghong, "External Difficulties and Challenges the New Leadership in China Is Facing: International Politics, Foreign Policy, and the Taiwan Issue," *Strategy and Governance* 3 (2003).

16. Wang Jisi, "China-U.S. Relationship at the Crossroads," in *China-United States Sustained Dialogue,* p. 68.

CHAPTER NINE

CHINESE COLLEGE STUDENTS' VIEWS OF AMERICA AFTER SEPTEMBER 11, 2001

Chen Shengluo

FROM MARCH 2000 TO OCTOBER 2001, interviews were conducted with more than 100 college students who attend nine different universities[1] in the cities of Beijing, Luoyang, and Fuzhou.[2] After a Chinese fighter plane collided with a U.S. scout aircraft over the South China Sea in April 2001, I met with several students to learn and record their reactions. After the events of September 11, 2001, I interviewed 28 students from eight universities[3] in Beijing. In 2003, I collected from academic salons, class discussions, and student essays and exams a great deal of information about students' reactions to the Iraq War.[4] These interviews and research were a part of my larger study of Chinese college students' image of the United States and how this image changes. Drawing on firsthand materials, I explored a subtle change in the Chinese college students' image of the United States after the events of 9/11 and beyond.

The research was divided into three parts: examination and analysis of Chinese college students' responses and attitudes to the events of 9/11; exploration of the reasons behind these responses; and description of the change in Chinese college students' image of the United States after 9/11.

STUDENTS' RESPONSES TO EVENTS OF SEPTEMBER 11

On September 11, 2001, terrorists made a surprise attack against the United States, which caused a great deal of grief and anger among most

Americans. Most Chinese college students, however, were immediately cheerful and excited because the United States—an abhorrent, overbearing, and arbitrary country in their minds—suffered an unprecedented heavy strike.[5] Following are initial student responses to the events of September 11:

> When the planes crashed into the World Trade Center, I really felt very delighted. Many things scattered, one corner of the building broke, suddenly the building fell down, and the other followed. I was very happy when I watched what had happened.[6]

> I heard the news on the radio. One building of the World Trade Center seemed to have fallen down. It was about midnight. Then the other building fell down, too. That night I was very excited, because someone gave a lesson to the United States. The news made me so excited that I was not able to use reason to think until the next day. The people in our bedroom joked with each other that night. It afforded general satisfaction to us.[7]

> While I was sleeping, people were talking about something and woke me. My first response was piquant. Despite the fact that thousands of people were killed, and the Pentagon was looking lost as well, I still thought it was good. . . . I don't think they have a right to complain about it. . . . They condemned bin Laden as a terrorist. They are terrorists, too. This is an eye for an eye.[8]

> I heard the news the next day around noon. A classmate came back to the bedroom and called, "Did you know someone bombed the Pentagon building?" Her face seems to be saying: "Sow the wind and reap the whirlwind." At first I felt very surprised. The United States is so powerful; who would dare bomb it? I had admiration for them.[9]

> Someone heard the news on the radio and told me. At that time I didn't think it was important . . . and I thought it was an ordinary bomb attack. The next day I found many people around the kiosk. . . . I knew an important thing had happened; the World Trade Center was destroyed. Good. I think it is a good thing. A person like bin Laden is admired. Who but him would dare to bomb the United States?[10]

Not only did most of the interviewees feel great delight, but many of their classmates had similar reactions. The interviewees described their classmates' responses as follows:

Most students in our bedroom were very happy. They were too delighted to put their eyes together. They lay on their beds, but they continued to talk about the event. After the Twin Towers fell down, they expected that more places in the United States would be bombed. The more severely the United States was bombed, the more excited they would be.[11]

In our bedroom, we all thought a hero had been born. The United States is too arbitrary; it should be taught a lesson. At that time we joked with each other. . . . The whole room burst into laughter again and again.[12]

The next day, a classmate of ours had newspapers and cried, "Extra! Extra! The U.S. was bombed!" We took the papers and read them. We found out that the World Trade Center was bombed. My response was the same as others. I was really very excited. I thought the bombing was right because of what the United States had done to other counties.[13]

To date, there has not been any national survey about student responses to 9/11, but based on these comments, it is easy to conclude that most Chinese college students felt excited and delighted about the events. They cheered the attacks and declared Osama bin Laden a hero for defying the United States.

WHY STUDENTS CHEERED EVENTS OF SEPTEMBER 11

When the United States was attacked, the Twin Towers as well as thousands of people burned to ashes within minutes. Most Americans were filled with deep sorrow. Why did most Chinese college students feel delight and cheer the terrorist attack? Is the United States an enemy of China?

Most Chinese college students have a bifurcated view of the United States. They see the United States as both a model and a potential enemy. In one image, the United States is an advanced and developed country, with admirable values. Many Chinese students yearn to go to the United States to study. In the second image, the United States seeks to contain, counter, besiege, and knock down China. In this view, the United States does not want China to get stronger and, in fact, views China as its enemy. Chinese students dislike U.S. foreign policy, especially its policy toward China, which they view as hegemonic. In short, while most Chinese college students admire the United States they also feel some hatred toward the United States because they think the United States sees China as its enemy or potential rival.[14]

An overbearing, unrestrained United States engenders hatred and rebellion. Since the 1990s, when the United States and China have disagreed over international issues,[15] the United States has been perceived in China to always prevail, getting what it wants and compelling China to endure policies China dislikes. As a result, Chinese college students have grown increasingly resentful of the United States.

One student offered his first response to the bombing of China's embassy in Yugoslavia:

> When I heard the news, I was so angry that I really hoped we would declare war on the United States, but I know we would never have the power to defeat it. . . . It seemed to me that someone had slapped us in the face, and not only did we have no way to strike back, but also we could not complain.

Another student added:

> I really think we are too weak in relation to the United States. The disparity between the two counties is too great in every way. Therefore, some actions of the United States can influence us greatly, but what the United States pays for these actions is negligible, while what we lose is great.[16]

Chinese college students had no outlet for their anger; therefore, many quietly hoped that one day someone might seriously attack the United States in a dramatic way. The events of September 11 met the hopes of Chinese college students and gave them a chance to release their anger and antipathy toward the United States.

It is evident that Chinese college students' acclamation of the events of September 11 is related to their image of the United States as a hegemon, as evidenced by the expressions the students initially used to describe the event. The delighted students passed the news around; the words they used were "the United States was bombed!" Implied in "the United States" is hegemony. The use of "bombed" instead of "attacked" is interesting and demonstrates that the Chinese students drew a connection between the events of September 11 and the bombing of the Chinese embassy in Belgrade. In the events of September 11, these students were not able to see the blood and tragedy of the deaths of innocent people; rather, they could see only an arrogant United States shivering with terror. September 11 gave students a chance to release their pent-up anger, and they felt compelled to enjoy their release of emotion. One student stated that it was "refreshing, very refreshing, . . . [that] someone punished the United States for us."[17]

Of course, some students had different responses. One student is from the Uygur Autonomous Region of Xinjiang, which has suffered terrorist attacks for many years. As a result of his personal experience, his reaction to September 11 was to condemn the terrorists. At the time, he criticized those who applauded the attacks and noted that China could be the next target of the terrorists. He said he was very angry and fought with other students on this issue, but none of them stood with him.[18] Another student, who likes Western culture but seldom concerns himself with politics, also rebuked the students who took pleasure in the U.S. misfortune. What he saw on September 11 was the deaths of many innocent people. He told the students, "You should not be delighted, you should think of the 9/11 events from the viewpoint of humanity and stand in silent tribute for the dead." But the students adamantly attacked his view and called him a traitor.

STUDENTS' IMAGES OF UNITED STATES CHANGED AFTER SEPTEMBER 11

The reaction of Chinese college students to the events of September 11 mirror the reactions of most Chinese people. The differences of ideology, social system, values, and national interests between China and the United States have been clear for more than 50 years; also evident is the unilateralism of the United States on international affairs. Consequently, most Chinese are used to looking at the United States with suspicion.

Chinese students and other groups in China, even some American studies specialists, paint an extreme and partial picture of hegemonic U.S. foreign policy.[19] They overstate the differences and conflicts between China and the United States in the fields of politics and diplomacy, rather than the areas of agreement in fields of economy and culture. This is a result of parochial nationalism in China. In the nationalist view, China-U.S. relations are a zero-sum game, a rival relationship between one superpower and an emerging power, in which both nations view each other as a threat. This parochial nationalism exists not only in the minds of some Chinese but also in the minds of some Americans.

At the time of the events of September 11, China's government immediately condemned the terrorist attacks. This strong statement reflected both moral support for the American people and the Chinese government's view that China-U.S. relations are deep and important over the long term, despite any differences the two sides might have. Both countries share a moral baseline of cherishing life and opposing terrorism. Both share a commitment to building global economic prosperity and maintaining world peace.

In addition to the government's clear support for the United States—in sharp contrast with the student reaction—other Chinese, especially in liberal intellectual circles, severely criticized the students for their *schadenfreude.* These two factors—the government response and the liberal intellectual criticism—made many students rethink their attitude toward September 11. They gradually realized that China and the United States share some values and interests. Moreover, the events of September 11 did not damage only the interests of the United States; they also damaged the interests of China and global security. The terrorist attacks proved that China-U.S. relations are not a zero-sum game. One student said:

> In my innermost thoughts and feelings, I really feel ashamed of my initial response. Because the United States had always opposed us, when it was bombed, I rejoiced and thought it was a good thing. . . . But my attitude changed subsequently. I began to think of the events from the viewpoint of humanity. The people in the World Trade Center were the same as us; they were lively people, . . . they had a happy life like us, but one day a plane crashed into them, and then they disappeared. . . . It is very pitiful. I have a lot of sympathy for the people.[20]

Another student experienced a similar change in attitude:

> At first, the information we had was not complete, so we thought about the issue merely from a narrow angle, a parochial nationalist viewpoint.[21]

In an effort to give students more information about the events of September 11, some universities began to play a special film, which changed many students' attitudes. One student described this change:

> At first, when we saw the scene of the plane crashing into the World Trade Center, we were very glad and applauded ardently. But as the film went on, when the scene of the buildings falling appeared, everyone was silent. Then, none of us saw the issue from that narrow viewpoint; we began to see it from the world as whole. . . . Reflecting on the fall of the Twin Towers, we asked ourselves, if our own relatives were in the building, what would we think of the terrorist attack? Our feelings of being spectators faded away and a feeling of comradeship gradually came forth. We not only regard the events as a matter for the United States, but also a matter for the whole world. . . . After we saw the film, our attitudes toward the events changed. We no longer applauded it. Although the terrorists attacked only the United States, what they wanted to damage were innocent people and the whole world.[22]

In classrooms, many teachers severely criticized the students who applauded the attacks and hoped they would look at it from a different viewpoint. A student said:

> On [September 12], our sociology teacher asked us, "I know many of you are very happy about the falling of the Twin Towers, but did you think about how many people were in the building? How many families suffered such an unexpected disaster?" What the teacher said made me rethink.[23]

Another student said:

> [Initially], I felt very happy. But subsequently, I thought it would be better if the events had not happened. The world economy declined after the events. As our teacher of a class entitled "Contemporary World Economy and Politics" said, "After the events, the United States will have to change its strategic target. It will pay more attention to military affairs than economic development, and the events will change the United States as well as the whole world."[24]

The events of September 11 affected some of the students' families, which also helped bring about a change in attitude. One interviewee said:

My mother works for a foreign trade company that produces clothing for the international market. After the events, my mother was out of work for a month, since the company lost the order from abroad. My mother told me our exports declined as the U.S. economy declined. Her words are strongly impressed on my mind. I knew that the events had a bad effect on China's economy.[25]

In some way, the events of September 11 revealed the nature of the China-U.S. relationship and gave prominence to a common enemy as well as the shared interests and values of the two countries. It led Chinese college students to go beyond their typical parochial, nationalistic point of view and rethink their image of the United States. To some degree, it also helped them to break through the bondage of their traditional hegemony and antihegemony thinking patterns and look at the U.S. role in the world from multiple angles. After September 11, Chinese college students not only saw the negative role of U.S. international behavior but also began to pay attention to the positive aspects of U.S. power: maintaining world order and making the world economy prosper, both of which serve the common interests of China and the United States. The events of September 11 slightly weakened the idea of the United States as a hegemonic figure in Chinese college students' minds and changed their image of the United States to a certain extent. Almost as soon as the image of the United States as a hegemon began to fade, however, it resurfaced and became even more powerful as a result of the war in Iraq.

Notes

1. The universities were Beijing University, Qinghua University, Beijing Normal University, Beijing Language and Culture University, Central University for Nationalities, Capital Normal University, China Youth University for Political Sciences, Luoyang University, and Fujian Normal University.

2. The author would like to thank the China Youth University for Political Sciences for financial support for this research. In addition, appreciation goes to university students Zeng Wenyuan, Wu Xiaojin, and Zhang Liang for their help with the interviews.

3. The eight universities are China People's University, Central University for Finance and Economics, University of International Business and Economics, China Agricultural University, Beijing Normal University, Beijing Health Science

University, China University of Political Science and Law, and China Youth University for Political Sciences.

4. Projects were entitled "Two Americas: Chinese College Students' Image of the United States," "The Views of Chinese College Students toward the Foreign Policy of the United States," and "The Four Factors Shaping Chinese College Students' Image of the United States."

5. This gleeful response of the students to the events of September 11 is well-known, but my interviews provide additional details.

6. Record of personal interviews (RPI) conducted by the author about events of September 11, 2001, p. 64.

7. RPI, p. 96

8. RPI, p. 84.

9. RPI, p. 61.

10. RPI, p. 64.

11. RPI, p. 3.

12. RPI, p. 97.

13. RPI, p. 82.

14. Cheng Shengluo, "Liangge Meiguo: Zhongguo Daxuesheng De Meiguo Guan" [Two Americas: How Chinese college students view the United States], *Qingnian Yanjiu* [Youth studies] (Beijing), no. 6 (June 2002): 1–10.

15. Issues that caused tension in the U.S-China relationship during this period include China's bid to host the 2000 Olympics, the *Yinhe* incident, arms sales to Taiwan, China's entry into the WTO, the bombing of China's embassy in Yugoslavia, the collision of U.S. and Chinese planes, Kosovo, the Middle East, and Iraq.

16. Chen Shengluo, "Zhongguo Daxuesheng Dui Meiguo Waijiao Zhengce De Kanfa" [Chinese college students' view of United States foreign policy], *Zhongguo Qingnian Zhengzhi Xueyuan Xuebao* [Journal of China Youth University for Political Sciences] (Beijing), no. 5 (2002): 9.

17. RPI, p. 33.

18. RPI, p. 2.

19. Cheng Shengluo, "Liangge Meiguo," pp. 6–7.

20. RPI, p. 2.

21. RPI, p. 64.

22. RPI, pp. 64–65.

23. RPI, p. 100.

24. RPI, p. 103.

25. RPI, pp. 102–103.

CHAPTER TEN

A MATTER OF BUSINESS PRINCIPLES

Ding Xinghao

CHINESE BUSINESSPEOPLE often say: "Kindness in doing business brings wealth." This maxim does not rule out fair competition based on equality and mutual respect, but it does discourage practices such as scheming, cheating, deception, and making money at the expense of other people. People who believe in this traditional saying often follow the principle of win-win. Thus, most traditional-minded Chinese businesspeople believe that statements such as "business means a battlefield" exaggerate the nature of business competition.

If this notion is stretched a bit further, it can also be argued that when merchants from two countries are doing business, they had better follow this principle as well. It will not only help establish friendship between the businesspeople themselves but also promote mutual understanding between the two countries. The development of human civilization and scientific technology has led to the establishment of various rules, which have been constantly improved, to guarantee normal business transactions on the basis of mutual benefits. These procedures ensure sustained growth in economic and trade cooperation between countries.

From the barter trade of the eighteenth century to the electronic business practices of today, the trade relationship between China and the United States has a history of more than 200 years. During most of the time before 1949, however, China and the United States were worlds apart in terms of economic strength—one being extremely backward and the other superbly advanced. In the late 1950s and 1960s, economic and trade ties between the two countries were cut off. During the 30-plus years since President Richard M. Nixon made his historic visit to China in 1972, the bilateral relationship has seen numerous ups and downs, but these decades also witnessed the rapid growth of economic and trade ties between the two nations. Chinese statistics indicate that the China-U.S. bilateral trade volume for 2002 reached $97.18 billion; U.S. statistics show that the trade volume between the two countries for 2003 amounted to $178.32 billion, more than 10,000 times the figure for 1972, which was $12.88 million. It is generally agreed that it is these ever-growing economic and trade ties between the two countries that have helped them survive one crisis after another. Clearly, the economic and trade relationship has played a positive and, indeed, indispensable role in the Sino-American relationship.

It should be pointed out, however, that the successful development of the economic and trade relationship has often been accompanied by conflicts and disputes. Such conflicts and disputes are neither avoidable nor surprising. However, Chinese entrepreneurs, whether they are from state-owned companies or from the private sector, all feel increasingly dissatisfied with the way Washington has tried to resolve these trade issues. They believe that, instead of holding discussions and negotiations with China on the basis of equality and mutual benefit, the Americans have too often and too readily resorted to domestic laws to deal with bilateral trade disputes, a process that not infrequently ends up imposing sanctions on China.

Nonetheless, as a whole, the overall image of the United States in the Chinese industrial and commercial community is quite positive. Chinese people in general, and Chinese businesspeople in particular, are fully aware that the United States is China's biggest export market and its most important trading partner. When it comes to trading, the Chinese business community is not only very eager to do business with its U.S. counterparts but also is quite enthusiastic about learning from them their advanced technology and sophisticated management skills. In fact, these Chinese businesspeople may even be interested in learning about the Americans' experience of relying mainly on their own domestic market to develop their economy some 200 years ago.

ENGLISH-SPEAKING AMERICANS

It is interesting that it was businessmen from Guangzhou, China, who first began the contact between Chinese and Americans. When the Americans on the *Empress of China* first arrived, Chinese merchants found that they spoke English, but they did not know the difference between Americans and the Britons who had come to China much earlier. When told that America and Britain were two different countries, Chinese people felt quite amused and treated the new arrivals very kindly. The Chinese business community found these newcomers to be gentle and friendly, unlike the Britons who often cheated, robbed, and despised the Chinese people. Thus, the first impression left by the Americans on the Chinese was a good one. Of course, Chinese merchants also wondered whether Americans would behave as viciously and cruelly as Britons if they came to Guangzhou more frequently.

Lin Zexu, a government official of the Qing dynasty who later became an anti-opium hero, and his colleagues also recognized this initial good impression. They believed Americans had come to China for trade and therefore treated China in a respectful way. Unlike the Britons, who flagrantly robbed Chinese people by exporting masses of opium to China to poison Chinese people and plunder the wealth of the nation, Americans simply engaged in barter trading.

Lin Zexu deserves credit for leading the way in introducing U.S. culture to China and thereby starting the Chinese people's process of understanding about the United States. Lin was in charge of the translation of *A Brief Account of the United States of America*, which introduced various aspects of U.S. society to the Chinese reading public in a relatively detailed fashion. Influenced by Lin Zexu, his colleagues and friends also began to offer their observations of the United States in an objective way, some of which were couched in flowery language. On the whole, they spoke highly of the fighting spirit of the people of North America in winning their freedom from British control. They also praised Americans for their smart strategy in seeking a French alliance against Britain. They reserved their highest praises, however, for the new political system established in the United States, and they expressed great appreciation for its new-style foreign policy. At one point, Lin Zexu and his colleagues even made an unambiguous suggestion that *Mei Yi* (America) and *Ying Yi* (Britain) be differentiated from each other and be treated differently, an idea that largely came from their contacts with U.S. and British businessmen.[1] It was only after the Opium War that Chinese merchants, government officials like Lin Zexu, and intellectual elites began to doubt their good impression of the United States. From that point on, Chinese people began to perceive that Americans were sly.

Chinese were most disappointed by those Americans who discriminated against, maltreated, and excluded Chinese people and who in the late nineteenth century even passed a law to ban Chinese labor. In 1848, the California gold rush led Americans to post advertisements in Guangzhou that promoted the idea that the United States was the richest country in the world—with big houses, good salaries, and ample food and clothing. It appeared that simply going to the United States was a fortune-making endeavor. Attracted by such advertisements, Chinese began to emigrate to the United States in large numbers, where they made substantial contributions to the United States in railway construction, road building, mining, and wasteland reclamation. However, what they got in return was persecution, expulsion, humiliation, and even death. In this sense, it was these Americans who ruined the initial positive image of Americans held by the Chinese people. Even President Theodore Roosevelt, not known for his sympathy toward the Chinese, acknowledged in his annual report to the U.S. Congress in 1905 that the exclusion of Chinese labor had inflicted enormous injustice upon the Chinese people and ultimately brought a burning shame upon America. This is a wonderful thing about Americans: sometimes they have the courage to admit their own mistakes.

THE AMERICA COMPLEX: LOVE AND HATE

In the history of the Sino-American relationship, Chinese people, including businesspeople, have always viewed America and Americans in a friendly way. Even when they are disappointed by or dismayed about the United States over certain issues, these feelings are often caused by U.S. government policy toward China. In other words, the Chinese people's opinion of the United States varies according to Washington's attitudes toward China and its China policy. On the one hand, preoccupied with its humiliating modern history and in an attempt to reassert itself, China tends to react strongly to any dispute with the United States. On the other hand, Confucianism promotes the idea that one should be grateful to others for kind help rendered in the past; such kindness should never be forgotten. The transformation of Chinese feelings from dissatisfaction to warm praise toward the United States during the Anti-Japanese War (1931–1945) is a case in point.

China's Anti-Japanese War began on September 18, 1931, when Japan invaded China. This invasion marks an important juncture in modern Chinese history because it threw the nation into a critical life-and-death struggle. China found itself in urgent need of international assistance, and it placed great hopes on the United States for moral and material support. To the disappointment of the Chinese, U.S. assistance did not come for a considerable amount of time. The Chinese understood that the United States was suffering from the Great Depression in the early 1930s, causing the country to remain idle when the war of resistance against Japan commenced in a country as remote as China. However, when the Japanese were using U.S.-made weapons to kill Chinese people in the late 1930s, there was little justification for the United States to continue its arms deals with Japan.

Even more intolerable, in 1941 the United States cut a compromising deal with Japan behind China's back, creating the Far East version of Munich at the expense of China. It is estimated that in 1937–1938 military supplies imported from the United States accounted for 55 percent of Japan's total military imports. In 1937, America's steel scrap export to Japan was 40 times that of 1931, representing 90 percent of Japan's total steel scrap imports of that year. In 1940, oil imported from the United States accounted for more than 50 percent of Japan's total oil imports. Of U.S. exports to Japan, 62 percent were military supplies used by the Japanese in their invasion of China. As late as October 1940, the Japanese were still flying new U.S. fighter planes to bomb and kill Chinese.[2] It is not surprising that Chinese people at that time became bitter about so-called American justice, humanism, and sympathy. It is traditional in China that even businesspeople, who love to make money, are not supposed to seek ill-gotten wealth. Some Chinese remarked sarcastically that "not all the crows in the world are equally black, for there is a difference in degree between them in blackness." In other words, both the United States and Japan were perceived to be imperialists, with the latter being fiercer and crueler than the former.

In 1941, in the wake of the Pearl Harbor attack, the United States declared war on Japan and the war in the Pacific began. As a consequence, the United States and China became allies in their fight against the Japanese fascists, leading to an immediate change in the Chinese view of the United States. On October 9, 1942, the United States repealed its unequal treaties with China; then, in early 1943, the two countries signed a new agreement, after which China's "America complex" returned. In this new twist, the United States changed itself from an imperialist to a friend in the minds of the Chinese people. During this period, virtually all Chinese—from government officials to people in the street, from Kuomintang to Communists—praised the United States highly. They cheered the Sino-U.S. friendship. With sentiment running high, the image of the United States soared in the minds of Chinese people.

SELF-INTEREST OR WIN-WIN

With 25 years of great strides in Sino-U.S. economic and trade relations, Chinese businesspeople from both state-owned and private-sector companies have gradually deepened their understanding and knowledge of their U.S. counterparts. In their eyes, U.S. businesspeople are both self-interested and susceptible to U.S. domestic politics. Therefore, for Chinese entrepreneurs with little experience with U.S. traits, it is unpredictable or even risky to do business with Americans. For example, in 2004, an election year in the United States, Sino-U.S. trade disputes were a hot issue. To appeal to domestic constituencies, the United States adopted special protective measures—temporary quotas on three types of textile imports—with regard to its trade with China. In addition, the United States made nine requests for investigations against China for dumping. The Bush administration continues to press China to revalue its renminbi (RMB). Among the first bills introduced in the Senate in 2005 was S. 14, which demands that China revalue its currency from the pegged-rate system; if China does not comply, the bill states, the United States will impose an additional 27.5 percent tariff on Chinese exports to the United States. A similar bill was introduced in 2004.

Of the many trade issues between the United States and China, the Bush administration has played up the issue of currency revaluation, mainly because of campaign politics and U.S. economic interest. The China-U.S. relationship in this instance has been devoid of the win-win principle observed in business deals. Because this situation is hurting Sino-American trade, it merits serious attention and judicious analysis.

First, the National Association of Manufacturers (NAM), a U.S. industry association, has vigorously lobbied the Bush administration to take measures to boost U.S. manufacturing and lower the U.S. unemployment rate. In response, the Bush administration has been seeking effective ways to promote the U.S. economy on the one hand, and provide for a scapegoat for its trade deficit, high unemployment rate, and declining manufacturing industry on the other. China and its currency valuation have filled that role.

The RMB exchange rate has no direct relationship with the U.S. trade deficit with China, much less with the decline of U.S. manufacturing. Take U.S.-Japan trade relations as an example. The Japanese yen has appreciated almost twice as much since the Plaza Accord of 1985; however, the U.S. trade deficit with Japan keeps mounting annually, and Japan has maintained its position as the nation with the largest trade surplus with the United States for years. Similarly, the euro has appreciated recently, but the U.S. trade deficit with the European Union still remains unchanged. These two cases make it very clear that even if the RMB does appreciate, it is not going to solve the problem of the huge U.S. trade deficit. The problem lies not in the value of the RMB but in the U.S. economy itself.

The RMB exchange rate should in no way be held responsible for the high rate of unemployment in the United States. Instead, the U.S. manufacturing sector is to blame. During the past several decades, U.S. manufacturers have shifted their investments overseas, building factories in developing countries, including China, and taking with them the job opportunities as well. This off-shoring does result in jobs for Chinese workers, but the number of Chinese workers employed by China-based U.S. companies represents only 1.5 per cent of the total workforce in China.

Second, the Bush administration has avoided the fact that U.S. factories in China sell their products back to the United States. Such a practice not only supplies U.S. consumers with cheap commodities but also increases U.S. government revenue, thereby indirectly creating job opportunities within the United States itself. On top of all this, U.S. corporations have reaped huge profits from doing business in countries like China. According to the American Chamber of Commerce in China, of the 254 U.S. companies in China interviewed, 75 percent reportedly made profits, among which 10 percent have made sizable profits.[3] Moreover, the rates of profit of U.S. companies in China in 2003 were higher than average global rates, a fact that will undoubtedly further encourage U.S. companies to shift their investments to foreign countries, including China.

To Chinese entrepreneurs and economists alike, a request by the United States for RMB appreciation is made purely out of U.S. economic interests rather than along the lines of the principle of win-win. In addition, such an attempt is also perceived to be a move on the part of the United States to shift its own economic problems to China, thus curbing the rapid growth of the Chinese economy. Some young Chinese economics scholars have argued in their publications that the Plaza Accord of 1985, which compelled the Japanese yen to appreciate, was in fact the first conspiracy plotted by the United States; forcing China to appreciate its currency would be the second. Quite a few Bush administration officials believe that China's rapid economic growth results from the Chinese government's regulation and control of the exchange rate and pegging the RMB to the U.S. dollar. It is assumed that when the RMB is devalued, in accord with the depreciation of the U.S. dollar, China's competitiveness in the world market will strengthen.

Furthermore, during the 1997 Asian financial crisis, China's insistence on maintaining the value of the RMB to ensure financial stability in the Asia-Pacific region was greatly appreciated by the United States. Now, as China is fulfilling its commitments to the WTO to further open up its domestic market and initiate financial reform, demanding the appreciation or free float of the RMB will not only weaken China's competitiveness in the world but also slow the influx of foreign capital to China. Worse still, it would likely cause financial instability in China, eventually putting the lid on the economic growth of China. Even viewed from the U.S. side, revaluation of the RMB will bring harm rather than good to the United States. It will hurt the interests of U.S. businesspeople who have invested and set up factories in China. It will also do harm to U.S. wholesalers and retailers engaged in Sino-U.S. trade. Finally, it will create adverse effects for U.S. consumers as a whole. Therefore, a revaluation of the RMB will only hurt one without bringing benefits to the other and will have a negative political impact on Sino-U.S. relations.

America's arrogance is not new, for Chinese people experienced it as early as the 1930s, also over a financial issue. At that time, Chinese elites and businesspeople respected the U.S. president, Franklin Roosevelt, not only for his efforts to set up an alliance with China after the Pearl Harbor attack to fight against the common enemy—Japanese imperialists—but also for his New Deal policy to save the U.S. economy. That said, the New Deal's silver policy caused a series of economic crises in China in the 1930s.[4]

At this time, China practiced a silver-standard monetary system, regarding silver as the lifeline of the country. However, while China was the largest consumer of silver in the world, it was not itself a producer. Therefore, after the implementation of Roosevelt's silver policy, China suffered a heavy outflow of its silver reserves, triggering a nationwide panic. Because of the severe shortage of silver in circulation, banks lost their credit, which led to a financial crisis. As a result, many Chinese banks closed down. Even Shanghai, then China's financial center, became "a land of misery." What followed in China was a general depression of the whole national economy, with agriculture in deep trouble and industry in total collapse. Indeed, the whole nation was plunged into the depths of enormous economic difficulty. Meanwhile, American silver-mine owners and silver dealers made a fortune. Through this silver policy, the Roosevelt administration helped the United States secure the dominant position in the world financial markets, paving the way for the United States to play its leadership role in the world. For this reason, in the 1930s it was generally agreed among Chinese merchants and intellectual elites that Roosevelt's silver policy shifted the U.S. economic losses caused by the Depression of 1929 to other countries, especially to China.

This review of an unpleasant episode in Sino-U.S. relations is not meant to settle old accounts. It is known to all that China is still a developing country, lagging far behind the United States in overall economic strength. It will take generations for China to catch up with the United States. Despite all this, however, China today is not the same as it was in the past, in terms of both its economic scale and its gross national product. While China needs America, America also needs China. So, in this world of growing globalization, mutual benefit may still serve as the supreme principle in conducting business between two nations. After all, a stagnant Chinese economy is no good to the U.S. economy. This view is widespread in the Chinese business community.

Notes

1. *Chinese Perspectives of America—A Historic Review* (Shanghai: Fudan Publishing House, November 1996).

2. Yang Shengmao, *A History of American Foreign Policy* (Beijing: People's Publishing House, 1991).

3. *2003 White Paper: American Business in China* (Beijing: American Chamber of Commerce, People's Republic of China, 2003), www.amcham-china.org.cn/publications/white/2003/en-1.htm.

4. In 1933, President Roosevelt approved the silver agreement and announced his administration's plan to raise the price of silver. Shortly afterward, the U.S. Congress passed a silver purchase bill and declared state ownership of silver. These moves caused quite a stir around the world. China, stunned by the news, saw an instant outflow of large amounts of silver. In 1933, China's silver exports were only 14 million RMB, but a year later, in 1934, exports of silver soared to 259 million RMB. Between 1934 and 1936, China's silver exports, legal and otherwise, totaled 1.29 billion RMB, representing half the total silver circulation of that period in China.

PART FOUR

AMERICAN VIEWS OF CHINA'S IMAGES

CHAPTER ELEVEN

THE MIRROR AND THE WALL
AMERICAN IMAGES OF CHINA

Terrill E. Lautz

WHEN WE AMERICANS look at China, we tend to see our own reflection, as in a mirror, or we perceive China as an obstacle or a wall. In both cases China is interpreted in terms of America's self-image and self-interest.

Why has it been so difficult to approach China clearly and objectively? To start with, the relationship between China and the United States has not been symmetrical. The United States sent missionaries, businesspeople, and soldiers to Asia, while the Chinese sent workers and students to the United States. While the United States steadily grew as a stable world power, China experienced prolonged upheaval and revolution. Despite their differences, the two countries developed an abiding mutual interest, alternating between attraction and repulsion.

U.S. reactions to China have been conditioned by long-standing assumptions, myths, stereotypes, emotions, hopes, and fears. Perceptions of China exist in three intersecting spheres—individual, public, and government. Private citizens; media, policy, and business groups; and the U.S. president and Congress interpret China in their own ways and for their own purposes. During the past 25 years, rapidly growing involvement with China has produced increasingly diverse and complex images. At the same time, a proliferation of special interest groups that advocate policies across the spectrum of U.S. politics has led to a fragmentation and intensification of images about China. Yet the tendency persists to be either fascinated or frightened by China and to see China as either open or closed.

Confusion and ambivalence over China is nothing new. Americans have always had two Chinas in their minds—a country that is big but weak, civilized but poor, cultured but authoritarian. Especially in Hollywood films, individual Chinese people have been portrayed as sophisticated but sinister, rational but inscrutable, competent but corrupt. For every example of Sino-American friendship and trust, there has been an equal measure of hostility and distrust, driven by a potent mixture of American altruism and racism. Historically, the debate about China has revolved around the ability of Americans to move China in the direction of U.S. values. A related issue has been whether China would emerge as a friend or a foe of the United States. Would China become a force for disruption and disorder or a force for peace and stability? Would China become Christian, capitalist, and democratic? Could Americans work to shape the outcome? Should Americans choose the mirror of engagement or the wall of isolation and containment?

The impulse to aid and transform China has its origins in the pre-1949 American Christian missionary movement, and it also grew out of the movement of Chinese students who came to U.S. universities for their education. The mutual admiration and respect created by many American missionaries and Chinese students contrasted with disdain for China's political and economic weakness, which was reinforced by a tragic history of discrimination against Chinese workers in the United States.

Flip-flops between positive and negative images have sometimes been dramatic. After the founding of the People's Republic of China in 1949, when the Western missionaries were labeled cultural imperialists and were told to leave, many Americans believed their hopes and dreams for a pro-American China had been betrayed—their mirror was shattered. The specter of a Soviet-Chinese alliance and the outbreak of war in Korea only seemed to confirm U.S. fears about the threat of Chinese communism—erecting the wall of the Cold War.

An entirely different mirror appeared during China's Cultural Revolution in the late 1960s, when some American intellectuals became convinced that Maoism offered solutions to age-old problems of poverty, health care, and social injustice. Deeply disillusioned with the

Vietnam War and racism in U.S. society, they looked to China as an exotic socialist utopia. In many ways this reaction was a revival of the old image of China as a place of beauty, order, spirituality, and morality, and it might be compared with the idealization of Confucian society by European philosophers in the eighteenth century.

AMERICAN PEOPLE, MEDIA, AND GOVERNMENT

Individual Americans who live or travel in China typically have positive reactions. Tourists, businesspeople, and students usually enjoy Chinese people, culture, and food. On the other hand, the general American public has mixed views of China. In a June 2002 opinion survey, a majority said that China's development as a world power is a threat to the United States. However, Americans do not favor isolating or confronting China. The same poll finds that "China is seen as practicing unfair trade by 53 percent of Americans, while 32 percent see it practicing fair trade. Only 32 percent would favor using U.S. troops to counter a Chinese invasion of Taiwan; 58 percent would oppose [the use of troops], even though 65 percent of Americans see Taiwan as a vital interest of the United States."[1]

One relatively new source of images comes from families in the United States that have adopted a total of more than 20,000 children from China since 1993. This unique vantage point has led many of these families to develop a deep interest in Chinese culture and social practices. One organization in the greater New York City area, Families with Children from China, embraces the idea of cultural internationalism and states, "Our mission is to provide a loving community that nurtures the adoption and parenting of children from China. We celebrate our cultural and racial differences to help one another fully integrate into our families the diverse roots, cultures and contexts from which we and our children come."[2] Another important source of images is the Chinese-American population in the United States, which has increased rapidly since 1965 but still numbers only about 3 million. Chinese-Americans from different parts of China, Hong Kong, and Taiwan transmit complex and diverse images across various sectors of U.S. society.

The news media have enormous influence on U.S. perceptions of China and sometimes induce tunnel vision. David M. Lampton has written:

> Television media, particularly in a crisis, focus viewer attention on a single issue and place; it is like looking at China through a straw. The view is real, but there is no peripheral vision. In June 1989, to most Americans, China equaled Tiananmen Square. Perceptually, there was no China beyond the range of the camera lens.[3]

The events of June 1989, replayed repeatedly on the nightly television news, led Americans to conclude that China's leadership had forcefully rejected a peaceful path to U.S.-style progress and development.

Negative perceptions of China cascaded during the 1990s. After the U.S. bombing of China's embassy in Belgrade in May 1999, the image of James Sasser, U.S. ambassador to China, peering from a U.S. embassy window broken by protesters in Beijing conjured an image of violent anti-Americanism. In April 2001, the detention of the crew of the EP-3 U.S. spy plane on Hainan Island produced images in the American press of China as a nation that flaunts international law. An April 3, 2001, editorial in the *Detroit Free Press* stated, "If China wants to be part of the world, China has to play by the world's rules. Those rules say give the plane back and return the crew unharmed."

More recently, China's slow response to the SARS epidemic in spring 2003 led the *New York Times* on May 19, 2003, to complain that "China's leaders have not yet fully grasped that Beijing's catastrophic mishandling of the health crisis is as much a political failure as a medical calamity. . . . China's ossified political system is out of sync with China's globalized, market-driven economy." China's first launch of a man into space in October 2003 raised concerns in some U.S. media about a new military threat. However, an October 19, 2003, editorial in the *New York Times* called it "a technological triumph for a still-developing nation" and said "this modest step should not reignite the global space race that died out with the end of the Cold War."

One entirely positive story in the American public eye has been Yao Ming's arrival in Houston in 2002 as a member of the National Basketball Association. Described as China's tallest ambassador, his modesty and good manners have earned him considerable praise in the sports pages of U.S. newspapers. Some have criticized Beijing for requiring Yao to turn over part of his salary to China, where he was trained in government-funded programs, but Yao himself has been above reproach and featured prominently in U.S. television commercials.

This brings us to the official realm of U.S. government policy toward China. Here, we see China policy driven, in part, by domestic partisan politics and fierce competition between the executive branch and the U.S. Congress. The contemporary competition to control China policy dates from 1979 when President Jimmy Carter negotiated diplomatic recognition of the People's Republic of China, and the U.S. Congress responded with the passage of the Taiwan Relations Act, which includes a provision for U.S. arms sales to Taiwan. Tensions between the two branches of government were exacerbated by the Tiananmen crackdown in 1989, after which Congress imposed sanctions even as the White House worked to preserve normal relations with China.

The administrations of Reagan, the first Bush, Clinton, and second Bush each moved eventually in the direction of emphasizing the longer-term strategic nature of U.S. interests in China, while Congress, as Robert Suettinger has observed, has been a watchdog and critic of China on human rights, trade, and military issues, seeing itself as the "guardian of values-based foreign policy."[4] Thus, U.S. presidents have seen U.S. interests mirrored in China, but the U.S. Congress has viewed China in opposition to those interests.

The Taiwan question remains the thorn in the side of official relations with China, reflecting the tensions between strategy and values. Each U.S. administration has reaffirmed the existence of "one China," hoping to maintain an ambiguous status quo. Meanwhile, Taiwan's evolution as a democracy has increased the willingness of the U.S. Congress to support Taiwan; and Taiwan, as seen in the reelection of President Chen Shui-bian in March 2004, has moved steadily away from the goal of reunification with China's mainland. The U.S. public's ambivalence about defending Taiwan may reflect an awareness of the potential dangers and difficulties of U.S. intervention. Yet, despite China's principle of noninterference, both the PRC and Taiwan now look to the United States for assistance in resolving their dispute.

NEW REALITIES AND CHANGING PERCEPTIONS

Since 2001, radical Islam has largely replaced China as a source of fear in the U.S. political imagination, and, as a consequence, the perception of China as a threat has diminished. Shared Chinese and American concerns about stability in Central Asia, West Asia, and the Middle East have not produced a new Sino-American strategic partnership but have led, by and large, to a suspension of negative judgments about China, at least for the time being. Islam's challenge to the United States places China in the potential position of mediating between East and West, moderating the extreme poles of orientalism and occidentalism. There is the risk, however, that China will be viewed in positive terms only so long as there is an enemy that brings Sino-American interests together, as was the case with Japan during World War II and the Soviet Union during the Cold War. History shows that a relationship determined by the principle that "the enemy of my enemy is my friend" is not a good basis for long-term stability.

At the same time, U.S. images of China have also benefited from the increased perception of North Korea as an irrational, unpredictable, and dangerous enemy whose behavior might be moderated by China. In general, there is a growing perception among scholars, policymakers, and the public of the PRC as a responsible and reliable regional and emerging world power, despite its periodic saber rattling about Taiwan. A shift toward understanding China in a multilateral and international context is just beginning to establish a new image of China.

These changing realities suggest that Americans and Chinese alike will need new ways to think about each other. Both nations will need to put aside the fantasies and obstacles of the past. Slowly but surely, Americans are taking down the mirror and the wall of China, realizing that China is neither an illusion nor a barrier.

Notes

1. Worldviews 2002 (joint project of the Chicago Council on Foreign Relations and the German Marshall Fund of the United States, June 2002), www.worldviews.org.

2. Families with Children from China, www.fccny.org.

3. David M. Lampton, *Same Bed, Different Dreams: Managing U.S.-China Relations, 1989–2000* (Berkeley: University of California Press, 2001), p. 278.

4. Robert Suettinger, *Beyond Tiananmen: The Politics of U.S.-China Relations, 1989–2000* (Washington, D.C.: Brookings Institution, 2003), p. 426.

CHAPTER TWELVE

U.S. SELF-IMAGE
PRIDE AND VULNERABILITY IN A CHANGING WORLD

Derek J. Mitchell

No INDIVIDUAL OR NATION LIKES TO RECEIVE CRITICISM. To the degree
that we have faults, we reserve the right to criticize ourselves—but we
will bristle if others agree with us.

Complex images and perceptions of the United States are a worldwide phenomenon; they are not restricted to the Chinese, although
some elements (discussed in other chapters of this volume) are specific
to China. However, it is not the perceptions themselves that are potentially the most troublesome challenge to the prospect of a sound bilateral relationship. More troublesome is any gap between those perceptions
and America's perception of itself. Such a gap can cause dissonance, often leading to resentment and friction.

This chapter examines America's image of itself, and it assesses the potential tensions that are caused by perceived dissonance with the views
toward the United States of others. It is of course difficult to encompass
all of America perfectly into generalized notions, as anyone's feelings
about anything, particularly one's country, are necessarily complex and
somewhat conflicted. Indeed, at the extremes of the political and soci-
etal spectrum, one may find fundamentally opposing ideological views
about the United States: the super-patriots or the "America: love it or
leave it" crowd on the right wing who will never find fault with any action of the United States simply by virtue of that action having been tak-
en by the United States; and, at the other extreme, those who cynically
view all U.S. action in the world as corrupt, illegitimate, or beholden to

craven (usually corporate) interests and, thus, see the United States as the primary source of all problems in the world.

Arguably, however, a dominant strain of opinion exists in the instincts of middle America—the majority of average U.S. citizens situated between the two extremes—that may be characterized in broad terms. Although divisions in American society during the Bush administration have grown, particularly over such issues as Iraq, in fact these cleavages may just prove the rule, as U.S. reactions reflect the tension within many Americans about how U.S. foreign policy may or may not clash with their self-image.

What follows then are, in good Chinese tradition, nine basic U.S. self-images that inform the way Americans view their place in the world. Note that the following commentary is an attempt to present subjective notions objectively and, thus, does not mean to suggest the author's personal views or offer an evaluation of the notions presented. It is expected that the reader's own images of the United States may differ from those presented here.

NINE U.S. SELF-IMAGES

Middle Kingdom. Ironic in the context of an examination of China, in fact Americans view their country as the real *zhongguo*—the center of the world politically, culturally, and economically. The rest of the world confirms this self-perception with its attention to U.S. popular culture, reflected through the enormous international popularity of Hollywood, the National Basketball Association, McDonald's, and more. The notion is further promoted through a dominant U.S. media presence, including CNN and Fox News, that educates the world daily about every U.S. preoccupation and trend. Americans who travel overseas or meet an international visitor at home are often surprised by, but have increasingly come to expect, the amount of knowledge foreigners have about even the smallest U.S. cultural events. Many Americans also are satisfied that they have all they need at home in the United States, and they believe that what they have others abroad want. Indeed, this concept is reaffirmed in the minds of Americans through the thousands of foreign citizens every year who seek to immigrate to the United States and who seek to do business or receive an education in the country.

Shining city upon a hill. Americans view the United States not only as a great nation but as the greatest nation—ever. When President Ronald Reagan quoted John Winthrop, likening the United States to a "shining city upon a hill," some Americans and others recoiled at the brash immodesty of such self-reverence. Yet in the heart of most Americans exists this same pride over the nation's unique founding principles of individual rights and its status as a beacon of freedom, democracy, and other humanistic values worldwide. This sentiment is reconfirmed in the American eye, again, by the foreign citizens who seek to live, work, or study in the United States and who seek to use the United States as a model for political, economic, or social change at home. Americans see their country as a land of opportunity like no other in history, both the most powerful and most humane even if sometimes flawed in its implementation of its high principles.

A corollary to such U.S. self-reverence is the deep and growing role of religion, particularly Christianity, in American life, and religion's connection to America's sense of itself either as essentially "missionary" in its instincts or simply divinely inspired. This religious sensibility among a growing number of Americans not only informs their view of others but also informs others' view of U.S. motivations and actions internationally, potentially complicating the effectiveness of U.S. initiatives if they are viewed as insensitive to other cultures or contexts.

Idealistic. The notion that the United States was not founded on ethnicity, culture, or other typical attributes of a nation but, instead, founded uniquely on an idea—democracy—has informed the U.S. view of the world and its place in it. For this reason, virtually from its founding, the United States has had a special view of itself and has sought to promote its founding ideals and principles around the world in an almost missionary way. In fact, democracy has been called America's "civic religion" for the depth to which Americans attach themselves to the principle. Indeed the missionary impulse runs deep in U.S. history, in both the figurative and the literal sense—the former through vocal promotion of democracy and human rights worldwide;

the latter in the form of a proselytizing Christian movement from the nineteenth century to the present that had a profound impact on the history of U.S. relationships around the world, and on U.S.-China relations in particular. Because the United States is a nation of immigrants, many of whom fled oppression in their home countries, the importance of promoting human rights is especially salient for Americans.

The corollary to U.S. exceptionalism and idealism is the view embedded in the nation's earliest days that the rest of the world—the Old World—embodies reactionary principles and that it is cynical and vaguely corrupt. This concept was the basis for George Washington's admonition in his farewell address to beware of "entangling alliances" with other nations, reflecting a view that the United States was different and should stay out of the old tensions, conflicts, and ways of thinking from which the new United States had an opportunity to escape, and to chart a new direction for international society. This sense of psychological exceptionalism was facilitated further by the physical separation of the United States from the Old Worlds of Europe and Asia by two vast oceans (which not incidentally also provided Americans a sense of security for most of the country's existence). Although much has changed in U.S. perspectives and engagement with the world since the late eighteenth century, wariness about Old World ways continues to inform U.S. instincts about international affairs.

Americans understand that U.S. foreign policy is not based purely on a sense of idealism or promotion of its values, nor should it be. But when the United States acts internationally, Americans are reluctant to acknowledge those ways in which they are normal practitioners of power politics. In the end, idealism and hard pragmatism coexist sometimes uncomfortably in U.S. policy and in the U.S. conception of this policy.

Well-meaning. Likewise, when the United States acts in the world, Americans believe the nation means not only to do well for itself but also to do good for the general interest. If there are excesses, they are anomalies. When U.S. foreign policy fails to live up to its ideals, it is not due to ill will but to the difficulties and responsibilities of leadership, the result of doing the best one can to balance competing interests and values in a difficult international environment. In this view, the United

States does not seek to dominate other countries or the world but, instead, seeks to make the world either (in the words of Woodrow Wilson) "safe for democracy" or (in the words of John F. Kennedy) "safe for diversity." Americans like to note that the United States has never sought territorial aggrandizement when victorious in war but, instead, has moved quickly to build up those societies it had defeated, as after World War II in Japan and Germany. U.S. engagement in Kosovo in the late 1990s, for example, was considered by Americans to be largely a humanitarian operation, as to some degree was the Iraq war to many. Thus, criticisms of the United States as "hegemonic" or engaging in "power politics" through such efforts grate against the sensibilities of many Americans about their national intentions.

Tolerant. Again, as a nation of immigrants from everywhere in the world—a self-described melting pot of different ethnicities, religions, and creeds—the United States considers itself an experiment in human political and social interaction, a proponent and exponent of diversity. While tolerance and fairness are far from being perfectly realized in U.S. society, a fact Americans fully recognize, they point to the Bill of Rights (freedom of religion, for example) and the Fourteenth Amendment to the U.S. Constitution (providing for equal protection under the law to all) as reflecting the essential nobility of the U.S. system and its aspirations. Indeed, the Latin phrase on every U.S. coin, *E pluribus unum* (Out of many, one), reflects a United States that views diversity and tolerance as being at the core of its national creed. This creed not only informs its perspective of itself domestically but also its conduct of international affairs.

Generous. Americans believe that, as the richest country in the world, they are generous in providing billions of dollars annually to help nations in need with development assistance, humanitarian aid, and emergency relief. Although Americans generally overestimate the actual level of U.S. international aid, the issue has never become deeply controversial. Americans may grumble at times—Why does the United States spend so much on other countries when we have so many problems here at home?—but at the same time they are proud of a perceived U.S. culture of voluntarism and note other reflections of a generous U.S.

spirit, such as the Peace Corps and other governmental and nongovernmental initiatives that promote development around the world.

Reluctant warriors. Despite engaging in multiple military conflicts throughout its history, including during the past decade, Americans view their country as peace loving and themselves as reluctant warriors. Americans may remember Woodrow Wilson won the presidency (twice) by vowing to keep the United States out of World War I, only to enter late after perceived provocation by the enemy. Isolationism was also a powerful force before World War II, and the Vietnam War was highly divisive and resulted in a postwar "syndrome."

History provides other lessons, however, that inform the way Americans view international affairs and the use of force. Americans are reminded often of the "lessons of Munich," that pre–World War II appeasement, withdrawal, and disengagement from the world did not prevent danger from coming to their shores but led instead to an international political and humanitarian disaster. With the revelation of the Holocaust and other atrocities, the phrase "never again" entered the American lexicon and psyche.

Even then, responsibility came only reluctantly after World War II: Korea, then Vietnam, for better or for worse, were steps taken to fulfill a role the United States assumed as "leader of the Free World" during the Cold War. Even in the aftermath of the Cold War, a sense grew in the minds of Americans: if we do not take action to safeguard international stability and prevent threats from gathering, who will? Hence Bosnia and Kosovo drew the United States slowly and reluctantly into military conflict, after much domestic debate and when it was evident that no one else was inclined to or capable of engaging the growing and increasingly apparent political and humanitarian crises. Afghanistan is viewed as a defensive war in response to the events of September 11, 2001. Many Americans agreed with President George W. Bush that Iraq was a "grave and gathering threat" and believed the United States had little choice but to handle it militarily in the near term to prevent development of a more dangerous threat later.

In each case, in the American mind, war was not the preferred course or an act of unprovoked aggression, but a defensive and unique responsibility of leadership. Indeed, despite these many military engagements over the past decade, one would be hard-pressed to find many average Americans who believe the United States is a warlike nation, or anything but a superpower reluctantly fulfilling its leadership role in an environment where others are unwilling or unable to handle international threats and maintain international peace and order.

Misunderstood. In the American mind, despite the best intentions of the United States as a responsible guarantor of international peace and security, the country is often misunderstood and unappreciated in much of the world for its efforts. To Americans, the carping against the United States is the easy criticism of those without the responsibilities of power but who benefit from the difficult choices and actions the United States must take to secure the peace. Those critics do not understand the complexities of international leadership, a role not necessarily of our own choosing. Although they may recognize that the United States makes errors and that questions about U.S. policies are legitimate, Americans bristle when the world challenges U.S. motivations in pursuit of its goals because, in the American mind, those goals are only honorable and best intentioned. The result of this discrepancy in perception is greater American cynicism about the world and affirmation of its own exceptionalism.

Vulnerable. Finally, despite enormous self-confidence as a nation and as the sole remaining superpower in the world, America nonetheless views itself as highly vulnerable and insecure, particularly after 9/11. The United States does not see itself—and in fact did not, even before 9/11—as omnipotent or omniscient simply because of its economic and military strength. After 9/11, Americans feel vulnerable arguably to a greater degree than they felt even during the Cold War. This mind-set was reflected in the U.S. public's support for the invasion of Iraq in 2003 and for the Bush administration's aggressive attitude toward the defense of U.S. interests overseas more generally. It is reflected also in the reelection of President Bush in November 2004: the public's comfort in the president's decisive conduct of national security and the war on terrorism were cited as key factors in gaining the decisive electoral support necessary for victory despite deep concerns over domestic issues and the war in Iraq.

To compound the sense of vulnerability, repeated failures of U.S. intelligence to both anticipate major international events affecting U.S. interests—the fall of the Soviet Union, nuclear tests in South Asia, and 9/11—and understand accurately what was happening in Iraq concerning weapons of mass destruction have shaken America's confidence in its knowledge and understanding of future threats. Facilitated by Hollywood movies and a reputation for innovation and high-tech gadgets, the U.S. national security establishment is viewed by much of the world as virtually omniscient and omnipotent in tracking and handling potential enemies, thus allowing the United States to undertake effective and deliberate foreign policy decisionmaking without fault.

The reality is not so simple or clean, however. In fact, the United States not only makes mistakes based on ignorance, misunderstanding, or incompetence like any other nation, but it is also becoming increasingly insecure about the reliability of its national security establishment, particularly its intelligence services, to protect it in a dangerous world. In turn, because the U.S. public no longer feels secure personally, they grant their government license to take extraordinary measures to defend them. This perspective affects America's view of the world and its role in it.

CONCLUSIONS

U.S. images of itself are complex, but, as one will note, overwhelmingly positive. To mitigate the sense of Americans as too arrogant or smug in their view of themselves, however, it should be noted that most citizens, even as they are fundamentally positive about their country and defensive about U.S. motivations, are at the same time highly self-critical about themselves and about whether U.S. policies and actions live up to their high standards. Deep in the U.S. consciousness, Americans recognize they do not live up to the best hopes and ideals of their self-image. Indeed, many Americans are cynical about their elected leaders and wary about their media; and most will reflect on apparent hypocrisy, inconsistency, and other shortcomings in their national policies. This is facilitated by an open society and a democratic tradition in the United States that encourages debate and criticism.

Nonetheless, Americans, like others, will be stunned when others react negatively to them even if, at times, they agree with the nature of the criticism. Indeed, like others, they often have trouble seeing themselves as others see them, and they assume that good intentions and the difficult responsibilities of leadership are enough of a defense to convince others to value the U.S. contribution. In fact, while the desire of most Americans to be admired and respected in the world will lead them to reflect on why others may view them differently, this self-reflection will not lead to support for policy changes simply because the world disapproves. In fact, international disapproval can be a badge of honor to many U.S. citizens, who have been bred in a culture of irreverence and defiance that dates back to the country's revolutionary origins and immigrant history.

Even as Americans maintain a sense that the United States has a special role to play in the world, they often resent the need to play this role at the cost of domestic affairs, particularly when the country's international actions are unappreciated by others. In moments of frustration, U.S. citizens will complain about the cost and burden of its internationalism, particularly that it does not prevent the loss of jobs, livelihoods, and even lives overseas. It is this attitude as well that leads to defensiveness bordering on defiance toward those who will criticize us from without.

Indeed, the gap between how others view the United States and how the United States views itself may become an essential complication to its bilateral relationships, none more than the relationship between the United States and China in the coming years. Beginning in the 1990s, the government of the People's Republic of China in its media and official public statements began to vilify the United States by ascribing, under the rubric of "hegemony and power politics," only the worst motives to U.S. actions. During the war in Kosovo, for example, no discussion of the humanitarian disaster unfolding in the territory or the complex motives for U.S. intervention was offered to the Chinese public through the media or otherwise. Instead, the official line consistently criticized the United States for a grand design of global domination.

One may understand the motives of the PRC government to attack such U.S.-led interventionism, given the applicability of intervention, humanitarian or otherwise, to the Taiwan issue. Nonetheless, indiscriminate and consistent vilification not just of U.S. actions but of U.S. motivations under favored slogans will not help mutual understanding or prospects for the relationship over the long term. Such phrasings will lead to U.S. resentment and suspicion of China's motives and intentions in return, to the detriment of the relationship.

In the end, the United States is a rather self-centered, proud, nationalistic, and self-reverent society with a sense of its own uniqueness and exceptionalism in world history—incidentally, all attributes that characterize China as well. At the same time, however, the United States can be a highly idealistic nation in its approach to the world, although often with a healthy dose of realpolitik and power politics, to be sure, in a way that China may find difficult to reconcile with its own historical principles and experience. Given the different histories and cultures, it may be difficult for China and the United States to understand fundamentally the unique perspectives each has on the world and itself. It is this perceptual gap, however, that needs to close over time through interaction and understanding, lest images—and self-images—overtake the best intentions of citizens on both sides to forge a lasting, positive relationship between these two "Middle Kingdoms."

INDEX

Page numbers followed by a t *or* f *refer to information in tables and figures respectively.*

Chinese Communist Party (CCP), 7, 27
Chinese Exclusion Act (1882), 5–6
"Chinese Images of the United States" (research project), 59–75
Chinese Repository (periodical), 3–4
Chomsky, Noam, 54
Christianity, 136
civil rights movement (U.S.), 11
civil war, 7–8
Clinton, Bill, 12, 35
CNN, 83
Cold War, 27, 128
Commager, Henry Steele, 44, 45
competition, economic, 40–41
Confucianism, 47
conspiracy theories, 21–22
Cuban revolution, 11
cultural diversity, 46, 53–54
Cultural Revolution, 11, 12, 27
culture, 11, 17–18; American, 68, 69*t*, 85
currency, 120–122

Dao Guang, Emperor, 47
de Tocqueville, Alexis, 49–50
Declaration of Independence (U.S., 1776), 48–49
deficit, trade, 70–71
democracy, 4, 35, 53, 66–67, 68*t*, 89, 136
Democracy in America (Tocqueville), 49
Deng Xiapong, 27, 29, 92, 96
Department of Homeland Security, 61
Dewey, John, 52–53
diplomacy, 3–9, 52–53. *See also* treaties

diversity, cultural, 46
double standards, 39
Dulles, John Foster, 11, 26

economic competition, 40–41
economy, American, 66–67, 67, 68*t*
economy, Chinese, 123–124
economy, global, 34–35, 112
education: of Chinese government officials, 25; higher, in U.S., 31, 63, 64*t*; of talents, 91–103
embassy bombing, 13, 43, 109
Emerson, Ralph Waldo, 47
Empress of China (ship), 3, 117
England. *See* Great Britain
Enron, 61
EP-3 crisis, 14, 43
Esperanto, 48
euro, 120–121
exchange rate, 120–121
extremism, 48–49

Fairbanks, John King, 79
feminism, 44–45
feudalism, 47
Flying Tigers, 7
foreign policy, 63–65, 64*t*, 65*t*, 66*t*, 81–82, 89–90, 99
freedom, 50–53
French Revolution, 49–51

Gang of Four, 27
Ge Honglin, 95
Ge Ming Jun (Zou), 47–49
generosity, 138–139
Germany, 39
Global Times (newspaper), 77
globalization, 32
government officials, 25–32

most-favored-nation status, 13
movies, 12
multiculturalism, 46, 53–54

National Association of Manufacturers, 121
NATO, 20, 36–37
new world order, 36
NGOs (nongovernmental organizations), 21–22
Nie Rongzhen, 96
nihilism, 48–49
North Korea, 72
nuclear arms, 61

Open Door Policy, 5, 11
Opium War, 4–5
optimism, 45

Panopticon, 51
paper-tiger analogy, 10
patriotism, 134
Pear Harbor, 120
ping-pong, 27
Porty, Richard, 49
poverty, 53
pragmatism, military, 38–40
preemptive strike, 31, 38–39, 61
presidential campaign, 2004, 61
pro-Americanism, 48
profiteering, 39–40
propaganda, 9–10, 18
prosperity, 34
public opinion, 88, 89–90

Qing dynasty, 3, 5, 49–50

radicalism, 44–46, 52
Reagan, Ronald, 136

realism, 44–46
religion, 21, 136
religious freedom, 83
religious policy, 18
Republic of China, establishment of, 6
research, 59–75. *See also* "Chinese
Images of the United States"
(research project)
revolution: American (1776), 48–
50; Chinese (1911), 47–50;
French, 49–51
The Rise and Fall of the Great Powers
(Kennedy), 64
Roosevelt, Franklin D., 7
Roosevelt, Theodore, 118
Rousseau, Jean Jacques, 47
Russian revolution, 19

Sandel, Michael, 52
SARS (sudden acute respiratory
syndrome), 79, 130
Saudi Arabia, 39
security, 16–17, 34
September 11, 2001, 13, 14, 29, 61,
106–113
Shalikashvili, John, 38
Sheng Xuanhai, 5
silver, 123
Smith, Adam, 49
Snow, Edgar, 27
social institutions, 21–22
socioeconomics, 17–18
sovereignty, 35, 36, 37
Soviet Union, 6–7, 9, 11; and Cold
War, 27; collapse of, 20; Stalinist
model of, 19–20
space exploration, 130
spy plane collision, 14
strategic thinking, 33–42

Strong, Anna Louise, 10
Sun Yat-sen, 6, 19
Suo Lisheng, 94–95
Super 301 sanctions, 34–35
superiority, 35–36

Taipin Rebellion, 3, 5
Taiwan, 17, 30, 69, 71t, 99–100,
    102–103, 129, 131
talents, 91–103
television, 31
terrorism. *See* September 11, 2001
Tiananmen Square, 12, 28, 130
Tocqueville, Alexis de, 49–50
tolerance, 138
Tongmeng Hui, 95
trade, 3–9, 70–71, 72t, 100, 115–
    124, 120–121, 120–124
The Tragedy of Great Power Politics
    (Mersheimer), 64
treaties, 4, 61. *See also* diplomacy

unilateralism, 17, 30–31
United Nations, 31, 39, 61
The United States and China (Fair-
    banks), 79

values, 35
Vietnam, 84
Vietnam War, 10–11, 26
Voice of America, 12
Wangxia Treaty, 4

Ward, Frederick T., 5
Washington, George, 4, 47, 137
Washington Monument, 4
Wealth of Nations (Smith), 49
Wei Jianxing, 96
Wei Yu, 94
Wei Yuan, 4
Wen Jiabao, 61
Williams, Samuel Wells, 3–4
Wilson, Woodrow, 6, 138
Winthrop, John, 136
women's rights, 44–45
World Bank, 34–35
World Trade Organization (WTO).
    See WTO
World War I, 6
World War II, 7, 119–120, 139
WTO (Word Trade Organization),
    34–35, 61, 70

Xie Qinaggo, 4
Xu Guanhua, 94
Xu Jiyu, 4, 47

Yao Ming, 130–131
Ying Huan Zhi Lue (Xu), 47
Yugoslavia, 37, 109. *See also* embas-
    sy bombing

Zhou Enlai, 96
Zou Jiahua, 96
Zou Rong, 47–50, 51

ABOUT THE CONTRIBUTORS

Chen Shengluo is an associate professor of contemporary world politics and China's economy, government, and politics at the China Youth University for Political Science. He received his Ph.D. from the Department of Government and International Studies at Hong Kong Baptist University, his M.A. from the Marxist School of Beijing University, and his B.A. in philosophy from Beijing University. Dr. Chen's major research interests include international socialism, Russian politics in the post–Cold War era, reform of Chinese state enterprises, and Chinese colleges' images of the United States.

Ding Xinghao is president of the Shanghai Institute of American Studies and is concurrently the director of the Institute of International Economy and Trade, Shanghai University of Foreign Trade. Professor Ding has had extensive interactions with U.S. foreign policy communities through various exchange programs, including visiting scholarships at the Brookings Institution in 1981 and 1990; at the School of Advanced International Studies of Johns Hopkins University from 1984 to 1985; at the Institute of International Studies at the University of California, Berkeley, in 1988; and at the Institute of East Asian Studies at Berkeley in 1990. His writings on U.S. domestic and foreign policies, Sino-U.S. relations, U.S. relations with the former Soviet Union, and the China-U.S.-Japan triangle have been published both in China and abroad. Professor Ding is also vice chairman of the Chinese Association for

American Studies and president of the Shanghai Association of American Studies.

Feng Changhong is a colonel in the People's Liberation Army (PLA) and a research fellow at the PLA's Military Science Academy. Col. Feng is also a part-time professor at Hainan Provincial University; and he is a member of China's International Relationship History Society, American History Study, the Chinese Military Law Institution, and the China Arms Control and Disarmament Association. Col. Feng attended Central China Normal University, the Chinese University of Politics and Law, Beijing University, and the National Defense University; and he holds a Ph.D. in strategic studies. He has authored numerous publications on Sino-U.S. relations and the international strategic environment.

Gong Li is a professor of international relations and vice director of the Institute of International Strategic Studies at the Central Party School of the Chinese Communist Party. He received his Ph.D. from the Central Party School in 1991, and he has published several books on Sino-American relations and Chinese foreign policy, including *Mao Zedong and the United States*.

John J. Hamre was elected CSIS president and CEO in January 2000. Before joining CSIS, he served as U.S. deputy secretary of defense (1997–1999) and under secretary of defense (comptroller) (1993–1997). As comptroller, Dr. Hamre was the principal assistant to the secretary of defense for the preparation, presentation, and execution of the defense budget and management improvement programs. Before serving in the Department of Defense, Dr. Hamre worked for 10 years as a professional staff member of the Senate Armed Services Committee. From 1978 to 1984, Dr. Hamre served in the Congressional Budget Office, where he became its deputy assistant director for national security and international affairs. He received his Ph.D., with distinction, in 1978 from the Johns Hopkins School of Advanced International Studies and his B.A., with high distinction, from Augustana College in Sioux Falls, South Dakota, in 1972, emphasizing political science and economics. He also studied as a Rockefeller Fellow at the Harvard Divinity School.

Hu Guocheng is a senior fellow and deputy director of the Institute of American Studies at the Chinese Academy of Social Sciences. He is concurrently an associate editor of the *American Studies Quarterly,* and editor in chief of the *Chinese Harvard Business Review,* both published in Beijing. Professor Hu has previously been an international fellow at the Kettering Foundation in Dayton, Ohio, and an academic visitor at the Imperial College in London. He served as a research fellow at the CASS Institute of World History, and a lecturer at Beijing Normal University's Department of History. He received a B.A. in history from Beijing University and did his postgraduate work at CASS. Professor Hu has authored numerous publications on modern U.S. economic history.

Terrill E. Lautz is vice president and secretary of the Henry Luce Foundation, where he also directs the Asia, Higher Education, and Henry R. Luce Professorship programs. Before joining the Luce Foundation in 1984, Dr. Lautz directed the field staff of the Yale-China Association and taught at the Chinese University of Hong Kong. Before living in Hong Kong, he worked with the Asia Society's China Council in New York and Washington, D.C. He graduated from Harvard College magna cum laude and received an M.A. in East Asian studies and a Ph.D. in history from Stanford University. After college, he served with the U.S. Army Medical Service Corps in Vietnam. He lived in Taiwan as a teenager and returned there for Chinese language training and research as a graduate student. Dr. Lautz has served as trustee and chairman of the Lingnan Foundation, trustee and secretary of the Yale-China Association, and member of the Research Advisory Board of the Australian National University's Research School of Pacific and Asian Studies. He has written and lectured on U.S.-China relations, Chinese and American mutual perceptions, higher education in China and Hong Kong, and financing for Chinese studies.

Li Xiaogang is director of the Department of U.S. Foreign Policy Studies at the Institute of American Studies at the Chinese Academy of Social Sciences. Dr. Li has been a research fellow at CASS since 1998. He received a B.A. from Shandong University and a Ph.D. from Nankai University. Dr. Li has previously taught at Shaanxi Normal University and was a visiting scholar at the Johns Hopkins School of Advanced International Studies. His main research interests are U.S. foreign policy and China-U.S. relations. He has published two books, *Refugee Policy* *and U.S. Global Strategy* and *Dream of Hegemony: American Global Strategy in the Post–Cold War Era* (co-authored with Director Wang Jisi of IAS). His articles have appeared in numerous journals, including *American Studies, World Affairs, World Economy and Politics,* and *Global Times.*

Li Xiaoping is executive producer at the assignment desk of China Central Television International (CCTV 9). She is concurrently a research associate at the Center for International Communication Studies at Qinghua University. Ms. Li has been a visiting fellow at the Center for Northeast Asia Policy Studies at the Brookings Institution and senior producer and program director of the International Division, Current Affairs Department, at CCTV. Ms. Li received a B.A. in Chinese Literature from Zhongshan University in Guangzhou and an M.A. in Television Studies from Leeds University in the United Kingdom. She has authored several publications and comparative studies on the Chinese television industry.

Lu Jiande is deputy director of the Institute of Foreign Literature, Chinese Academy of Social Sciences, and author of *Doctor Zhivago and Other Essays* (San Lian Press, 1996) and *Fragments of Broken Systems* (Peking University Press, 2001).

Carola McGiffert joined the CSIS International Security Program in May 2002. Previously she was the senior policy adviser for the New Democrat Network (NDN), where she helped build support among congressional Democrats for permanent normal trade relations for China and China's accession to the World Trade Organization. Before joining NDN, Ms. McGiffert was vice president of the Newmarket Company, a consulting and information services firm. From 1997 to 1998, she was vice chairman of the international trade practice at Mayer, Brown & Platt. Ms. McGiffert worked in the Clinton administration from 1993 to 1997: in the Office of the U.S. Trade Representative, the Department of Commerce, and at the White House. In 1992, she was the deputy research director for the reelection campaign of Senator Christopher Dodd (D-Conn.). Ms. McGiffert received an M.A. in international economics and Chinese studies from the Johns Hopkins School of Advanced International Studies and a B.A. from Wesleyan University. She is a term member of the Council on Foreign Relations.

Derek J. Mitchell joined the Center for Strategic and International Studies in January 2001, as senior fellow for Asia projects in the International Security Program. In this position, Mr. Mitchell is responsible for managing all Asia-related studies conducted in the program. Mr. Mitchell was appointed as special assistant for Asian and Pacific Affairs, Office of the Secretary of Defense; and he also served as senior country director for China, Taiwan, Mongolia, and Hong Kong during 2000–2001, and as director for regional security affairs from 1998 to the end of 2000. During his term at the Defense Department, he also served as country director for Japan and senior country director for the Philippines, Indonesia, Malaysia, Brunei, and Singapore. Mr. Mitchell was the principal author of the Defense Department's 1998 East Asia strategy report. Prior to joining the Department of Defense, Mr. Mitchell served as senior program officer for Asia and the former Soviet Union at the National Democratic Institute for International Affairs in Washington, D.C.

Wang Jisi is dean of the School of International Studies at Peking University. Until recently, he was director and a senior researcher of the Institute of American Studies at the Chinese Academy of Social Sciences in Beijing. He is concurrently director of the Institute of International and Strategic Studies at the Party School of the Central Committee, the Communist Party of China; a guest professor at the PLA's National Defense University; vice chairman of the China Reform Forum; and president of the Chinese Association for American Studies. He is a founding member of the Pacific Council on International Policy in Los Angeles, an international council member of the Asia Society in New York City, an advisory council member of the Center for Northeast Asian Policy Studies of the Brookings Institution in Washington D.C., an adviser to the East Asian Security Program of Stanford University, an international adviser to the Institute of Global Conflict and Cooperation at the University of California, and an adviser to the Asia Center at Harvard University. Professor Wang has taught at Beijing University's Department of International Politics; was a visiting fellow at St. Antony's College, Oxford University; was a visiting scholar at the University of California, Berkeley; and was a visiting associate professor at the University of Michigan, Ann Arbor. He taught at Claremont McKenna College in California as a Freeman Professor of Asian Studies and taught and did research at the Singapore Institute of Defence and Strategic Studies as an S. Rajaratnam Professor. Professor Wang received an M.A. from Beijing University, and he has published numerous works on international relations theory, U.S. foreign policy, Chinese foreign policy, and China-U.S. relations.

Zhao Mei is a senior fellow and director of the editorial department at the Institute of American Studies of the Chinese Academy of Social Sciences. She is a managing editor of *American Studies Quarterly,* which is published jointly by the Chinese Association for American Studies and the Institute of American Studies of the Chinese Academy of Social Sciences. Before joining the Chinese Academy of Social Sciences in 1990, she taught at Beijing Normal University. She was an international fellow at the Kettering Foundation in Dayton, Ohio. Her scholarly interests cover U.S. culture and social history.